Better Homes and Gardens®

Junior Cook Book

FOR BEGINNING COOKS OF ALL AGES

Spoon a generous amount of the zesty sauce over the hot dogs in a bun when you serve Saucy Hot Dogs (page 18). Be sure to make plenty because everyone will want 'seconds.'

CONTENTS

Our seal assures you that every recipe in *Junior Cook Book* is endorsed by the Better Homes and Gardens Test Kitchen. Each recipe has been tested for family appeal, practicality, and deliciousness.

COOKING
can be so easy

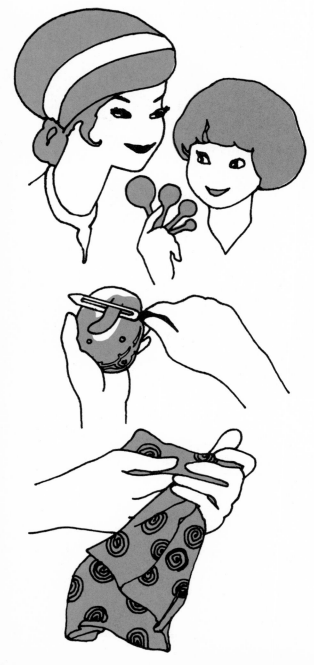

Talk it over with Cook, Sr.

She'll think it's wonderful to have a Junior Cook—you can count on her for help. Ask your Mother to show you how to use the range and some of the small appliances. Or maybe you already know? Talk over your recipe with her. Make sure that you are not out of some of the ingredients before starting the recipe. Also make sure you have the utensils you need; check utensil identification on pages 8 and 9 before you begin.

Peel and chop this way

Cut away from yourself when you use a vegetable peeler. Hold the vegetable in one hand, the peeler in the other. Watch out for the fingers. It's a good idea to check with Mother before you use a knife; she will show you which knife to use for the job. If you're slicing, dicing, or chopping, do the job on a wooden cutting board so you won't damage the countertop. Always check to see that 'all's clear.'

About spills

And now have a look at yourself—you're spotlessly clean, of course, and your hair is neat and brushed back. How about wearing a spanking clean apron to protect your clothes? Wipe your hands very dry after you wash them. Wet hands are slippery—regular 'butter fingers.' Use paper toweling to wipe up spills right away so someone doesn't slip and fall.

It's fun to learn to make sizzly hamburgers, thick chocolate shakes, beautiful gooey rolls—all of the delicious foods you love to eat. And think how proud you will be to cook meals and snacks for your family and friends. Cook your favorites the simple and safe way by following these helpful tips.

Watch out for ouches!

Sure as a pot's hot, you'll say *ouch* if you don't use a potholder. Steady the handle with a potholder while you stir. When you take hot dishes or a baking sheet out of the oven, use a potholder in each hand. With potholders, pull the oven rack out *a little way* to make it easier to lift out the hot pan from the oven. Set hot pans on a wire rack, a hot pad, or a countertop that heat does not hurt.

Cool hand, hot pot

Stir a hot mixture on the range with a wooden spoon or a metal spoon with a wooden or plastic handle. An all-metal spoon gets hot; hot enough to burn your fingers. If you leave the range for just a minute, remember to turn the handle of the pan so no one will bump the pan and spill it when walking by. Also use a wooden spoon for beating; it plays the part of your silent partner in the kitchen.

How to put in a plug

Be sure your hands are dry when you plug in or disconnect an appliance. When you are through using the appliance, take hold of the plug and pull straight out. Don't pull on the cord—you may loosen the wires inside the plug. Remember— always unplug the appliance cord from wall *first*—then take cord from the appliance. Store the cord with the appliance so that the cord is easy to find.

Cooking terms

Stir—To mix around and around with a spoon or fork. Usually, you stir with a spoon, but use a fork to stir pastry.

Whip—To beat rapidly. Use rotary eggbeater to whip cream or to beat egg whites till light and fluffy. Beating adds air.

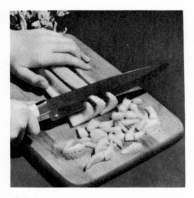

Chop—To cut in pieces the size of peas with a knife or food chopper. Chop foods on a wooden cutting board.

Bake—To cook in the oven.

Baste—To pour or brush liquid over food while it cooks.

Beat—To make mixture smooth by mixing fast with beater or spoon.

Blend—To mix the ingredients until smooth and uniform.

Boil—To cook until liquid is so hot it bubbles hard.

Broil—To cook directly over coals or under heat in broiler.

Chill—To place in the refrigerator to lower temperature.

Combine—To mix ingredients.

Cream—To beat until smooth, soft, and fluffy.

Cube—To cut food into pieces with 6 sides that are usually larger than ¼ inch.

Cut in—To mix shortening with dry ingredients, using a pastry blender or two knives.

Dice—To cut food into small cubes of same size and shape.

Dot—To put small pieces of one food on top of another, such as butter over pie filling.

Flour—To coat with flour.

Fold—To mix ingredients gently with a rubber spatula, whisk, or spoon. Cut down through mixture, go across bottom of bowl, then up and over, close to surface of mixture.

Fry—To cook in hot fat.

Garnish—To decorate finished dish with colorful food to make it look pretty.

Grate—To rub on a food grater that breaks up the food into very fine particles.

Grease—To rub pan surface with fat to prevent sticking.

Knead—To fold, turn, and press dough with heel of hand.

Ladle—To dip and serve liquid with a ladle.

Melt—To make liquid by heating.

Mince—To cut or finely chop food into tiny pieces.

Mix—To stir foods together.

Peel—To remove outer skin.

Pit—To take out the seeds.

Scald—To heat milk just below boiling point. You'll see tiny bubbles around the edge.

Shred—To cut into thin strips with a shredder.

Sift—To put dry ingredients (flour) through sifter or sieve.

Simmer—To cook in liquid over low heat so bubbles form slowly.

Toss—To mix foods lightly.

Well—A hole made in dry ingredients in which you pour liquid.

Measuring up to good cooks

Successful cooking adventures depend on correct measuring. It pays to be accurate. Always use special measuring cups and measuring spoons—not the kind you use when you eat.

Liquids

A glass measuring cup has a 1- or 2-cup mark below rim so you won't spill. Cup has a lip. Place cup on counter to measure liquids. Bend down and watch as you pour.

Shortening

Pick cup or spoon that holds amount the recipe calls for. Pack shortening so there won't be any air left in cup or spoon. Level off top with straight edge of a knife.

Dry ingredients

Pick cup or spoon that holds amount recipe calls for. Fill to overflowing. Level with knife. Careful—don't pack ingredients.

Brown sugar

Pick the right size cup. Fill with brown sugar. Push down hard with spoon. Add more; pack down. Level off top with knife.

Cooking utensil

Utensils you need for measuring

Utensils you need for mixing

DRY AND LIQUID MEASURING CUPS

MEASURING SPOONS

RUBBER SPATULA

METAL SPATULA

MIXING BOWLS

ROTARY EGGBEATER

ELECTRIC MIXER

RUBBER SPATULA

WOODEN SPOON

PASTRY BLENDER

Utensils you need for basic preparation

PARING KNIFE

TABLE KNIFE

VEGETABLE PEELER

GRATER

CUTTING BOARD

CAN OPENER

FRUIT JUICER

VEGETABLE BRUSH

SIEVE

SIFTER

identification

Utensils you need for cooking on top of the range

SAUCEPAN

SKILLET

DOUBLE BOILER

WOODEN SPOON

PANCAKE TURNER

POTHOLDERS

Utensils you need for baking

BAKING SHEET

PIE PAN

SQUARE PAN

ROUND CAKE PAN

LOAF PAN

OBLONG PAN

PANCAKE TURNER

MUFFIN PAN

POTHOLDERS

ROLLING PIN

chapter 1

Beverages

Root beer float

1 Take a glass the size you want. Open root beer with bottle opener. Fill glass ⅓ full with root beer.

2 Stir several spoonfuls of ice cream into root beer. Pour glass ¾ full with root beer. Top with ice cream.

You'll need:

Chilled root beer

Vanilla ice cream

Take out:

glass

bottle opener

spoon

Leave plenty of room in each glass of Root Beer Float for that final spoonful of vanilla ice cream. Easy does it! Not too big or it will run over. Offer spoons and straws to those enjoying this all-time favorite beverage.

Frosty lime float

You'll need:

1 cup
chilled
pineapple
juice

⅓ cup
lime juice

⅓ cup sugar

1 pint lime
sherbet

1 16-ounce
bottle
chilled
lemon-lime
carbonated
beverage

Take out:

pitcher
spoon
measuring cup
glasses
bottle opener
ice cream scoop

1 Put pineapple juice, lime juice, and sugar in pitcher. Add ½ cup lime sherbet; stir mixture till smooth.

2 Pour ½ cup juice into each of 4 glasses; add 1 scoop sherbet to each glass. Fill with lemon-lime beverage. Serves 4.

Serve Frosty Lime Float to your friends out in the back-yard. Set these cool refreshers on a large serving tray along with some colorful stirrers. Big scoops of lime sherbet floating on top will please everyone.

Tutti-frutti-ice
SPARKLE

You'll need:

1 1-ounce package
each: unsweetened
orange, lime, and
cherry-flavored soft
drink powder
Sugar
Water
Chilled
lemon-lime
carbonated
beverage
Lemon slices, halved

Take out:

3 large pitchers
or bowls
measuring cups
spoon
3 ice cube trays
with dividers
glasses
bottle opener

1 Mix *each* flavor of soft
drink powder with ⅔ cup
sugar and 4 cups water. Pour
into separate ice cube trays;
freeze till solid.

2 To serve, put one ice cube
of *each* flavor in a big glass.
Fill the glass with lemon-lime
carbonated beverage. Add
lemon slices for garnish.

Drop colorful orange, lime, and
cherry-flavored ice cubes
into tall glasses, and fill with
sparkling lemon-lime beverage
to make this refreshing summertime drink, Tutti-Frutti-Ice Sparkle.

Eggnog

You'll need:	Take out:
1 egg	mixing bowl
2 tablespoons sugar	rotary eggbeater
Dash salt	measuring spoons
1 cup milk	measuring cup
½ teaspoon vanilla	glass

1 Break the egg into a mixing bowl. Beat egg with a rotary eggbeater until the egg looks smooth and thick.

2 Add sugar and dash salt to egg in bowl. Beat with rotary eggbeater until sugar and salt are dissolved.

3 Carefully beat milk and vanilla into egg mixture with rotary eggbeater. Serve eggnog immediately. Makes 1.

Orange FIZZ

You'll need:

1 cup orange juice
¼ cup sugar
Ice cubes
2 7-ounce
   bottles
   chilled
   ginger ale
Quartered
   orange slices

1 Combine orange juice and sugar; chill. Put ice cubes in 4 tall glasses. Add ¼ cup juice mixture to each.

2 Gently fill glasses with ginger ale. Stir once or twice. Add quartered orange slices for garnish. Serves 4.

Take out:

measuring cups
small pitcher
spoon
glasses
bottle opener

14

Rich chocolate SHAKE

1 Place about 5 big spoon-fuls of vanilla ice cream in a shaker or jar.

You'll need:

Vanilla ice cream	2 tablespoons chocolate syrup	½ cup milk

Take out: spoon, covered shaker or jar, measuring spoons and cup, glass or mug

2 Add chocolate syrup to ice cream in shaker. Mix a bit with spoon. Add the milk.

Use more ice cream to make Rich Chocolate Shake extra thick.

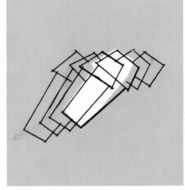

3 Cover shaker tightly with lid; shake hard. Pour in glass. This makes 1 milk shake.

CIRCUS TIME

lemonade

You'll need:	1 6-ounce can frozen lemonade concentrate	Cold water	Ice cubes	Lemon slices
Take out:	can opener, pitcher, spoon, glasses			

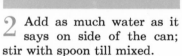

1 Open the can of frozen lemonade concentrate. Empty the concentrate in tall pitcher.

2 Add as much water as it says on side of the can; stir with spoon till mixed.

3 Put ice cubes in glasses. Fill with lemonade. Add a lemon slice to each glass.

Lemonade Variations

Pink Lemonade is easy. Just color the Circus Time Lemonade with a few drops of red food coloring. The use of pink ice cubes makes this lemonade even prettier. To make pink ice cubes, freeze one 12-ounce bottle of strawberry pop in an ice cube tray. This makes enough cubes to chill 1 recipe of Circus Time Lemonade. Or, tint the lemonade pink with maraschino cherry juice from the jar, and add Fancy Ice Cubes (page 17) with red cherries in them.

Old-Fashioned Lemonade is like Mother makes. Dissolve 1 cup sugar in 1 cup cold water and 1 cup lemon juice. Add 4 cups cold water. Serve over ice. Makes 6½ cups. *Hot Buttered Lemonade* makes you warm inside. In saucepan heat ½ cup sugar, 3 cups boiling water, 1 or 2 tablespoons butter, and 1 teaspoon grated lemon peel till sugar dissolves and mixture boils. Add ½ cup lemon juice. Pour into heatproof mugs; top with thin lemon slices. Serves 4.

Creamy COCOA

You'll need:

⅓ cup unsweetened cocoa powder ⅓ cup sugar Dash salt

½ cup water 3 ½ cups milk 4 tablespoons marshmallow creme

Take out: measuring cups, saucepan, spoon, measuring spoons, potholder, cups or mugs, ladle

Ladle hot, Creamy Cocoa into lively, colorful mugs to make any-time party time. Melt marshmallow creme atop each serving and pass with a plate of crunchy cookies to your family or friends.

1 Mix cocoa, sugar, salt, in pan; stir in water. Cook and stir to boil; boil 1 minute.

2 Stir in milk. Heat *just* to boiling. Remove pan from heat with potholder.

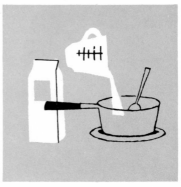

3 Ladle cocoa carefully into 4 cups. Top each with 1 tablespoon marshmallow creme.

Beverage Ideas

Fancy Ice Cubes

Put plain soda pop in the special party class with these fancy coolers. To make them, freeze a red or green maraschino cherry in each of the ice cubes in an ice cube tray. Or, use a pineapple chunk, a lime slice, or a strawberry. First, wait until the ice has started to form around the sides and bottom of the cubes. Then, add the fruit of your choice. This keeps the fruit centered in the cubes. Use the ice cube coolers in glasses when you serve drinks.

Beverage Trimmers

Stirrers: Whirl a peppermint stick in mugs of cocoa or cold glasses of milk to add a pretty mint-flavored surprise.

Stir a cinnamon stick in hot or cold apple cider to add a delicate, spicy flavor.

Toppers: Creamy whipped cream or marsh-mallow creme gives a party touch to cups of hot cocoa or ice cream sodas. Tint the whipped cream with food coloring, if desired.

Garnishes: Cut one slash from center to rind of an orange or lemon slice. Use slit to hang over the rim of a glass of refreshing lemonade or other cold fruit drink.

Fresh fruit slices, such as orange or lemon, add a colorful, festive tang to a fruit drink.

For beverage coolers, freeze ice cubes, using your favorite soft drink or fruit juice.

Perch a small sprig of mint leaves atop a cooling summertime drink.

Thread a few pieces of fresh fruit onto the drinking straw of a colorful fruit drink.

Birthday Party Punch

Your friends may want more than one glass of this frothy ice cream drink at your birthday party. Scoop 1 quart of your favorite flavor of sherbet into a large punch bowl. Carefully add three 28-ounce bottles chilled lemon-lime carbonated beverage. Ladle into punch cups. Makes 25 to 30 one-half cup servings.

Whipped Cream Topper

Here's how to make this rich topper to perfection every time. Set a small mixing bowl and a rotary eggbeater in the refrigerator till they are cold. Put 1 cup chilled whipping cream in chilled bowl. Beat with rotary eggbeater till whipped cream mounds and holds its shape when you lift the rotary eggbeater out of the bowl. Add 3 tablespoons sugar and ¼ teaspoon vanilla to whipped cream. Beat with rotary eggbeater till sugar and vanilla are blended. Keep mixture cool in refrigerator.

Cherry Soda

Instead of stopping at the ice cream shop, treat your friends to a soda at home right after school. You can use your favorite soft drink powder for different flavors. Combine one envelope unsweetened cherry-flavored soft drink powder and 1 cup sugar in pitcher. Stir in 2 cups cold milk. Pour into 6 to 8 tall soda glasses. Using 1 quart vanilla ice cream and one 28-ounce bottle chilled carbonated water, add scoops of ice cream to glasses. Carefully pour the chilled carbonated water into each glass. Stir slightly. Makes 6 to 8 servings.

Two-Tone Sparkle

Surprise the family with this two-colored dazzler at breakfast. Into each of 6 small glasses, pour ¼ cup chilled apricot nectar. Tip the glass; *very slowly* pour ¼ cup chilled cranberry juice cocktail down the side of the glass. Do not stir.

Apple Cider Snap

This is a good treat to serve in the fall when school starts. Fresh doughnuts taste terrific with the hot drink. In saucepan combine 1 quart apple cider *or* apple juice and 2 tablespoons red cinnamon candies. Heat and stir till candies dissolve and cider is hot. Serve in mugs. Thinly slice an apple crosswise to float on top.

chapter 2

Sandwiches and Breads

Hot dogs

You'll need:

6 hot dogs   6 hot-dog buns

Softened butter or margarine

Take out:

saucepan and lid
potholder
knife
table knife
tongs

1 Fill saucepan half full with water. Bring water to a boil; add hot dogs. Cover saucepan and let water return to boiling again. Turn off heat. Remove pan from heat. Let hot dogs stand in hot water 8 to 10 minutes. Leave lid on.

2 Cut hot-dog buns in half lengthwise, if necessary. Butter both sides of the buns with butter or margarine. Use tongs to remove the hot dogs from saucepan. Put hot dogs in buns with tongs. Serve with mustard, catsup, and relish.

Saucy Hot Dogs

You'll need: 1 tablespoon shortening, ½ cup chopped onion, one 14-ounce bottle catsup, ¼ cup water, ¼ cup pickle relish, 1 tablespoon sugar, 1 tablespoon vinegar, ¼ teaspoon salt, dash pepper, 10 hot dogs, 10 hot-dog buns.

Take out: measuring cups, measuring spoons, knife, skillet, spoon.

Heat shortening in skillet. Cook onion in shortening; add other ingredients *except* buns. Simmer, covered, 15 minutes. Serve in buns.

Hamburgers

1 Use measuring cup to measure ⅓ cup ground beef for each patty. Shape 6 hamburger patties with your hands.

2 Ask Mother to help you heat shortening in skillet. Brown patties over medium-high heat 5 minutes per side.

3 Sprinkle patties with salt and pepper. Spread buns with butter or margarine. Serve hamburgers in buns.

You'll need:

1½ pounds
    ground beef
2 tablespoons
    shortening
Salt
Pepper
Softened butter
    or margarine
6 hamburger
    buns

Take out:

measuring cup
measuring spoons
skillet
pancake turner
potholder
knife

Top each with a slice of tomato and cheese; broil a few minutes.

BAR-B-Q-Burgers

You'll need: 1 pound ground beef, ½ cup chopped onion, ½ teaspoon salt, dash pepper, ¼ cup water, one 10½-ounce can condensed chicken gumbo soup, 1 tablespoon catsup, 1 tablespoon prepared mustard, 8 hamburger buns.

Take out: skillet, paring knife, measuring cups, wooden spoon, measuring spoons, can opener, potholder.

In skillet cook beef and onion together until meat is lightly browned. Stir frequently with wooden spoon. Add the remaining ingredients *except* hamburger buns to mixture in skillet. Cover; simmer over *low* heat gently for 30 minutes. Stir occasionally. When mixture is done, spoon into buns. Serve at once.

Grilled cheese sandwich

Offer to make a tasty Grilled Cheese Sandwich for each member of the family. Keep the sandwiches warm in the oven while you are toasting the last one. Then, serve them immediately with the family's favorite soup and relishes, such as crisp carrot or celery sticks.

You'll need:	Take out:
1 slice process cheese	measuring spoons
2 slices bread	small skillet
1 tablespoon butter	pancake turner
or margarine	potholder
	knife

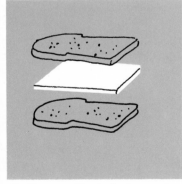

1 Put a slice of cheese between 2 slices of bread. Use slices of dark or light bread for variety. Or, use light bread for one side of the sandwich and dark bread for the other.

2 Melt butter in skillet over *low* heat. Toast sandwich in butter till it is lightly browned. Watch carefully so it doesn't burn. Peek under by lifting with pancake turner.

3 Flip the sandwich over with the pancake turner. Take your time; do it carefully. Toast sandwich till the second side is as brown as the top. Cut sandwich in half.

Lunch box heroes

You'll need:	Take out:
½ cup butter or margarine	measuring cup
2 teaspoons prepared mustard	small bowl
French rolls	measuring spoons
Sliced luncheon meats	spoon
Sliced process Swiss cheese	knife
Lettuce leaves	table knife

Make these super sandwiches to take along with you the next time you go on that all-day fishing trip with Dad. You will both enjoy eating Lunch Box Heroes.

1 Allow butter to stand at room temperature to soften. Put softened butter in small bowl. Add mustard to butter. Use spoon to blend butter and mustard together.

2 Cut French rolls in half lengthwise with knife. Use table knife to spread each half with some of the butter mixture. Save the rest to use on other sandwiches.

3 Layer meat, cheese, and lettuce between roll halves. If you are taking the sandwich in a lunch box, carry lettuce separately in a plastic bag. Add lettuce before eating.

Egg in a bun sandwiches

You'll need:

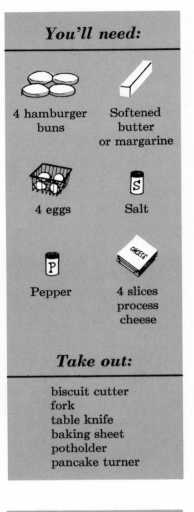

4 hamburger buns

Softened butter or margarine

4 eggs

Salt

Pepper

4 slices process cheese

Take out:

biscuit cutter
fork
table knife
baking sheet
potholder
pancake turner

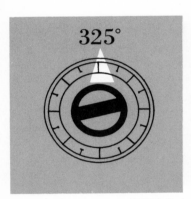

1 Set the oven at 325°. Get the serving plates ready so you can whisk the hot sandwiches right to the table.

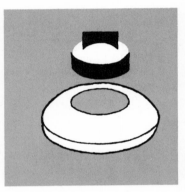

2 Put biscuit cutter in center of a hamburger bun. Cut down 1 inch. *Don't cut through bottom of bun.* Repeat.

3 Carefully lift the bun circles out with a fork. Butter inside of holes in hamburger buns well with butter.

4 Place buns on baking sheet. Break an egg into each hole in the buns. Season eggs with salt and pepper.

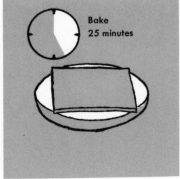

5 Place in oven. Bake for 25 minutes. Now, top each sandwich with a slice of cheese. Bake about 5 minutes more.

Gooey rolls

You'll need:	Take out:
2 tablespoons sugar 2 tablespoons all- purpose flour 2 tablespoons softened butter or margarine 2 tablespoons honey 6 brown-and-serve rolls Nut halves	small bowl measuring spoons spoon baking sheet table knife potholder

375°

Bake about 15 minutes

1 Set oven at 375°. Put sugar, flour, butter, and the honey in a small bowl. Mix ingredients till blended.

2 Put rolls on a baking sheet. Spread honey mixture on top of the rolls. Then, arrange nut halves on top of each roll.

3 Place baking sheet in the oven. Bake about 15 minutes. Serve the rolls while hot. Don't worry about leftovers.

You'll need:

1 slice bread   Softened butter or margarine

¼ cup sugar   1 tablespoon ground cinnamon

Take out:

toaster, table knife, measuring cup and spoons, shaker

Cinnamon toast

1 Toast bread in toaster. Spread toast at once with softened butter or margarine.

2 Combine sugar and cinnamon in shaker. Sprinkle some of mixture on toast.

Cinnamon twists

Pretty Cinnamon Twists are fun to make, and they taste so good for breakfast, served warm from the oven. Use your own ideas for ways to twist them into different shapes.

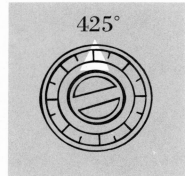

425°

You'll need:	**Take out:**
2 tablespoons butter or margarine	small saucepan
¼ cup sugar	bowl
1 teaspoon ground cinnamon	ruler
1 package refrigerated biscuits (8 biscuits)	baking sheet
1 tablespoon chopped walnuts	potholder

Take out: small saucepan, bowl, ruler, baking sheet, potholder, pancake turner

1 Set oven at 425°. Melt butter in small saucepan. Remove from heat. Combine sugar and cinnamon in bowl.

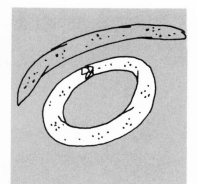

2 Roll each biscuit into a 9-inch rope. Use a ruler to measure. Pinch ends of ropes together with fingers to seal.

3 Dip biscuit circles in melted butter, then in sugar-cinnamon mixture. Twist each biscuit to form a figure 8.

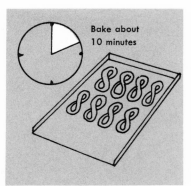

Bake about 10 minutes

4 Place biscuits on baking sheet. Sprinkle with nuts. Bake 8 to 10 minutes. Remove twists with pancake turner.

Perfect French toast

You'll need:

2 eggs

½ cup milk

¼ teaspoon salt

4 or 5 slices bread

3 tablespoons shortening

Powdered sugar

Maple-flavored syrup

Take out:

bowl
rotary eggbeater
measuring spoons
    and cup
spoon
shallow pan
skillet
pancake
    turner

Nothing tastes better for breakfast than hot French toast served with sweet maple syrup.

1 Break eggs in bowl. Beat with rotary beater till eggs are fluffy and blended. Stir in the milk and salt.

2 Pour egg mixture into a shallow pan. Dip in the bread slices. Make sure both sides are coated with egg.

3 In skillet heat shortening. Brown bread on both sides in fat. Sprinkle with sugar; pass syrup.

flip-flop pancakes

Have plenty of butter and a pitcher of warm honey or syrup ready. Then serve hot, golden Flip-Flop Pancakes right from the griddle to your hungry family. Prepare one of the special pancake toppers for a weekend morning feast.

You'll need:	Take out:
 Packaged pancake mix Shortening	bowl measuring cups measuring spoons wooden spoon skillet or griddle waxed paper pancake turner potholder

Build a breakfast tower with pancakes and Cherry Sauce. Save extra sauce to serve over ice cream.

1 Look on pancake mix package for directions. Mix batter according to directions to make 12 to 14 pancakes.

2 Now, rub the skillet or griddle lightly with a little bit of shortening placed on a piece of folded waxed paper.

3 Heat the griddle. If drops of cold water skitter and dance around on griddle, it's hot enough to cook pancakes.

4 Pour 3 tablespoons to ¼ cup batter onto the griddle. Measuring helps you keep all the pancakes the same size.

5 Pancakes get bubbly on top when ready to turn. Easy over. Lift with turner to see when bottom is brown.

Cherry Sauce

You'll need: ¾ cup sugar, 2 tablespoons cornstarch, ¾ cup orange juice, one 20-ounce can pitted tart red cherries, red food coloring.
Take out: measuring cups and spoons, 2-quart saucepan, spoon.

Mix sugar and cornstarch in saucepan; stir in orange juice. Add cherries and food coloring. Stir over medium heat till bubbly. Boil for 2 minutes. Serve warm.

Special Pancake Toppers

Honey Butter: Mix ½ cup softened butter and ¼ cup honey. Beat with rotary eggbeater till light and fluffy.
Orange Sauce: In small saucepan combine ½ cup butter or margarine, 1 cup sugar, and ½ cup frozen orange juice concentrate. Bring to boil; stir occasionally.
Cinnamon Candy Syrup: Combine ½ cup light corn syrup, ½ cup maple-flavored syrup, and 3 tablespoons red cinnamon candies in small saucepan. Cook over low heat, stirring till candies melt.

Peanut Butter Waffles

You'll need: 1 cup packaged pancake mix, 2 tablespoons sugar, ⅓ cup chunk-style peanut butter, 1 egg, 1 cup milk, 2 tablespoons cooking oil.
Take out: measuring cups, measuring spoons, bowl, spoon, waffle baker.

Ask Mother to heat the waffle baker. Combine ingredients in bowl; beat almost smooth. Pour *half* the batter in baker; close lid. Waffles are done when steam stops escaping from baker or indicator light signals. Makes two 9-inch waffles.

Cherry fill-ups

Early-bird breakfast eaters will be delighted with warm, cherry-filled biscuits. Pour glasses of milk to drink with these.

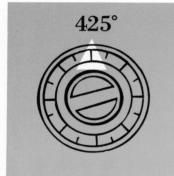

425°

1 Set the oven at 425°. Ask Mother to open the biscuits for you. Arrange biscuits in a round pan so they nearly touch.

You'll need:	*Take out:*
1 package refrigerated biscuits	9 × 1½-inch round pan
Cherry jam	teaspoon
1 egg	bowl
2 tablespoons sugar	rotary eggbeater
2 tablespoons milk	measuring spoons
	pastry brush
	potholder
	pancake turner

2 Press a tiny dent in the center of each biscuit with your fingertips. Fill the dent carefully with 1 teaspoon jam.

3 For the glaze, break the egg into a bowl and beat smooth with a rotary eggbeater. Beat in sugar and milk.

Bake 10 minutes

4 Brush on egg with pastry brush. Bake 10 minutes. Use potholder to remove. Remove biscuits with turner.

Jelly muffins

You'll need:	Take out:
Shortening	muffin pan
1¾ cups sifted all-purpose flour	waxed paper
	flour sifter
¼ cup sugar	measuring cups and spoons
2½ teaspoons baking powder	bowls
¾ teaspoon salt	small skillet
⅓ cup shortening	rotary egg-beater
1 egg	spoons
¾ cup milk	rubber spatula
Jelly	potholder

1 Set oven at 400°. Lightly grease muffin cups with a bit of the shortening on waxed paper, or use paper bake cups.

2 Measure the sifted flour in a small bowl. Add sugar, baking powder, and salt. Sift all of these into a large bowl.

3 Put ⅓ cup shortening in small skillet; heat until it is melted. Remove skillet from the heat. Let it cool slightly.

4 Break the egg into a small bowl. Beat with rotary egg-beater till fluffy. Add milk. Then, add melted shortening.

5 Make a well in center of flour mixture. Add all the milk mixture. Stir *only* until dry ingredients are moistened.

6 Fill the muffin cups half full. Drop 1 teaspoon jelly in the center of each cup. Bake about 25 minutes. Makes 12.

Flaky biscuits

You'll need:	*Take out:*
Packaged biscuit mix Milk *or* cold water	measuring cups mixing bowl fork rolling pin pastry cloth or board biscuit cutter baking sheet potholder pancake turner

1 Set oven at 450°. Check biscuit mix box for how much mix and milk *or* water to use. Stir ingredients till dough follows fork around bowl.

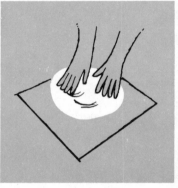

2 Dust rolling pin and pastry cloth with biscuit mix. Put dough on cloth; knead 8 times (knead by folding, turning, and pressing with heel of hand).

3 Roll dough out with rolling pin to ½ inch thick. Dip biscuit cutter in biscuit mix before cutting. Cut biscuits. Repeat; dip cutter each time.

Bake 8 to 10 minutes

4 Put biscuits on ungreased baking sheet. Put biscuits in oven. Bake 8 to 10 minutes. Tops will be a golden brown. Remove biscuits with turner.

Split open a hot Flaky Biscuit just as it comes out of the oven. Set a generous pat of butter or margarine on top so it will melt down into the hot bread. Serve with your favorite jelly or jam. Tastes so good, you will want to eat one more.

Sandwich and Bread Ideas

Easy Tuna Sandwiches

Make these for you and your friends on a hot summer day when Mom is busy. In a small bowl combine one 6½- or 7-ounce can tuna, drained; ¼ cup mayonnaise or salad dressing; and ¼ cup chopped celery. Mix thoroughly. Spread over buttered bread slices. Serve with tall glasses of cold milk and cookies for dessert.

Salad-in-a-Sandwich

Spread one slice of toast with deviled ham and one slice with mayonnaise or salad dressing. Place two thin tomato slices and a lettuce leaf atop the ham. Cover with second toast slice, mayonnaise side down. Cut sandwich into quarters. Serve with potato chips and milk.

Tea-Party Sandwiches

Use cookie cutters in fancy shapes to cut slices of bread into pretty cutouts. Use a table knife to spread cutouts with softened butter or margarine. Be sure to spread the butter to the edges of the bread. Then, spread the bread with jelly or pimiento cheese spread. Put two cutouts of the same shape together, filling sides together, to make a sandwich.

Pigs-in-a-Blanket

Can you guess what the pigs are? Hot dogs, of course! Unroll dough from 1 package refrigerated crescent rolls (8 rolls). Separate dough along perforation. For each sandwich, place hot dog at shortest side of triangle and roll up to opposite point. The ends of the hot dog will peek out from biscuit blanket. Put sandwiches on an ungreased baking sheet, point side of roll down. Bake at 450° for 10 to 12 minutes. Biscuits should be lightly browned. Serve hot.

Cocoa Toast

Make cinnamon toast a new way. In a bowl mix together 3 tablespoons sugar, 1 tablespoon unsweetened cocoa powder, and ½ teaspoon ground cinnamon; sprinkle over slices of hot, buttered toast, using a spoon or a shaker.

Pineapple Prize Pancakes

These are as easy to make as plain pancakes, but they'll earn you the 'good cook' title. To make these treats, press 1 slice of well-drained pineapple into each circle of pancake batter on the griddle. Before the cake is ready to turn, hide the pineapple under a bit of batter. To do this, spoon about 2 teaspoons of batter over fruit. Now flip the pancake over and bake on the other side. Serve with warm syrup and softened butter.

Peanut Butter S'Mores

Split hamburger buns and spread each bun half with chunk-style peanut butter. Top with a big dollop of marshmallow creme. Place the bun halves on the broiler pan and broil until the marshmallow topknot is lightly browned. These taste best served at once.

Garlic Bread

Slice French bread in 1-inch slices *without cutting through* the bottom crust. Mix ½ cup softened butter with ¼ teaspoon garlic powder. Spread garlic butter between slices of bread and over top of loaf. Wrap loaf in foil and heat at 350° for 10 to 15 minutes. Serve bread in a basket.

Crunchy Breadsticks

Cut refrigerated biscuits in half. Roll each half into a pencil-thin stick about 4 inches long. Dip sticks in milk and then in slightly crushed crisp rice cereal. Place on greased baking sheet. Bake the breadsticks at 450° till sticks are lightly browned, about 10 minutes.

chapter 3

Main Dishes

Speedy chili

You'll need:			**Take out:**	

½ cup chopped onion

¼ cup chopped green pepper

1 pound ground beef

Take out:

knife
measuring cups
saucepan
wooden spoon
can opener
measuring
   spoons
potholder

2 8-ounce cans tomato sauce (2 cups)

1 16-ounce can kidney beans (2 cups)

1 teaspoon salt

1 teaspoon chili powder

1 Cook and stir onion, green pepper, and ground beef in saucepan till meat is lightly browned. Spoon off excess fat.

2 Stir in tomato sauce; cook over low heat for 5 minutes. Stir in kidney beans and salt. Cook till heated through.

3 Stir in 1 teaspoon chili powder. Taste. Add a little more if you like it zippy. Serve with crackers. Serves 6.

Cook about 5 minutes

Gather your four favorite people together and serve them Cheeseburger Round Steak and Peppy Potatoes. Both the meat and potatoes bake in the oven at the same time.

Cheeseburger round steak

You'll need:

2 tablespoons all-purpose flour
¼ teaspoon salt
1 pound beef round steak, cut ½ inch thick
2 tablespoons cooking oil
½ cup water
1 teaspoon instant minced onion
2 slices process American cheese, halved

Take out:

small bowl
measuring cup and spoons
meat mallet
knife
10-inch oven-going skillet with lid

Peppy Potatoes

You'll need: 1 package seasoned coating mix for chicken; ¼ teaspoon salt; 4 unpeeled potatoes, cut in 1-inch wedges; melted butter. *Take out:* measuring spoons, baking sheet.

Pour coating mix and salt in mix bag. Dip potatoes in melted butter; shake in bag. Place potatoes on well-greased baking sheet. Bake at 325° for 55 minutes.

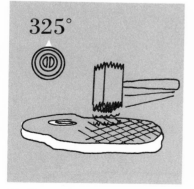

1 Set oven at 325°. Combine flour and salt in small bowl. Pound meat to ¼-inch thickness with meat mallet.

2 Cut meat into 4 pieces. Carefully heat oil in skillet. Brown the meat *slowly* in hot oil. Add water and onion.

3 Cover skillet; bake in oven for 1 hour. Add more water, if needed. Top with cheese; heat, covered, to melt cheese.

Everyday drumsticks

You'll need:	Take out:
1 pound ground beef	bowl
1 egg	measuring spoons
1 teaspoon salt	wooden spoon
12 single saltine crackers	plastic bag
6 wooden skewers	rolling pin
3 slices bacon	waxed paper
	baking pan
	kitchen shears
	potholder
	pancake turner

Individual meat loaves made with ground beef are shaped around wooden skewers and called Everyday Drumsticks. The whole family will enjoy this new and different mealtime idea.

1 Set oven at 450°. Put ground beef, egg, and salt in bowl. Stir till mixture is well blended. Divide into 6 parts.

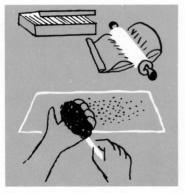

2 Put crackers in bag; crush with rolling pin. Put cracker crumbs on waxed paper. Shape meat around skewers.

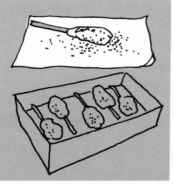

3 Roll meat drumsticks in saltine cracker crumbs on waxed paper. Place drumsticks in a greased baking pan.

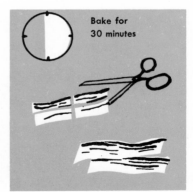

4 Cut each bacon slice in half lengthwise and crosswise. Put 2 pieces atop each drumstick. Bake 30 minutes.

Oven-fried chicken

You'll need:	Take out:
½ cup butter or margarine 1 4-ounce package potato chips ¼ teaspoon garlic salt Dash pepper 1 2½- to 3-pound ready-to-cook broiler-fryer chicken, cut up	measuring cup small skillet potholders rolling pin measuring spoons waxed paper jelly-roll pan metal tongs

1 Set oven at 375°. Melt butter or margarine in skillet over *low* heat. Use potholder to remove pan from heat.

2 Crush potato chips with rolling pin before opening the bag. Mix potato chips with garlic salt and pepper.

3 Dip chicken pieces in melted butter, then roll in potato chip mixture. Keep the mixture on waxed paper.

4 Place chicken on jelly-roll pan, skin side up. Pour rest of melted butter and crumbs over chicken. Bake 1 hour.

Use metal tongs to remove crispy Oven-Fried Chicken from the jelly-roll pan to a colorful, napkin-lined basket for serving at the table. The crunchy potato chip coating is easy to make and tastes so good. Plan to serve four people with this recipe.

SAUCY
spaghetti

You'll need:	Take out:
1 pound ground beef	skillet
½ teaspoon instant minced onion	wooden spoon
¼ teaspoon salt	measuring spoons
¼ teaspoon dried oregano leaves, crushed	can opener
Dash pepper	
1 19½-ounce can spaghetti in tomato sauce with cheese	
Green pepper and onion rings	
Grated Parmesan cheese	

If you like, use the electric skillet to make Saucy Spaghetti. Sprinkle the spaghetti mixture with Parmesan cheese, and serve with Garlic Bread (page 31). This recipe serves four.

1 Brown the meat in skillet (electric skillet 350°). Stir. Spoon off fat. Add onion, salt, oregano, and pepper.

2 Use can opener to open the canned spaghetti. Pour spaghetti into the browned meat. Stir with wooden spoon.

3 Top with green pepper and onion rings. Cook, covered, over *low* heat for 5 minutes. Sprinkle with cheese.

You'll need:	6 cups water	2 teaspoons salt	1 7¼-ounce package macaroni-and-cheese dinner	3 tablespoons butter or margarine	¼ cup milk	1 sprig parsley

Take out: large saucepan, measuring cups, measuring spoons, potholder, spoon, large sieve, serving dish, fork

Macaroni and cheese

1 Put water and salt in large saucepan; heat to boiling. (The water is boiling when it bubbles and 'rolls' in pan.)

2 Add macaroni to boiling water. (Save out envelope of cheese.) Stir. Return water to boiling; boil 7 minutes.

3 *Carefully* pour water and macaroni into a sieve. Do this over sink. Be careful not to get burned by hot steam.

4 Put the hot macaroni in a serving dish. Add butter and milk. Mix all ingredients lightly, but well, with fork.

5 Sprinkle the cheese from the envelope over macaroni. Mix lightly. Add parsley sprig. Serve at once. Serves 4.

Peppy frank pizza

Surprise your friends with two of their favorite foods—hot dogs and pizza—both prepared in one meal. Thin slices of hot dog bake on top of Peppy Frank Pizza along with pickle relish and a lot of cheese.

You'll need:	*Take out:*
2 cups packaged biscuit mix	measuring cups
½ cup water	bowl
1 5½-ounce can pizza sauce (⅔ cup)	spoon
4 hot dogs	rolling pin
½ cup shredded process American cheese	12-inch round pizza pan
¼ cup pickle relish	can opener
3 green pepper rings	paring knife
	pizza cutter

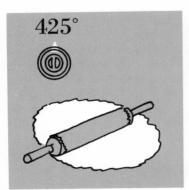

425°

1 Set oven at 425°. Mix biscuit mix and water. Shape into ball on floured surface; knead 6 times (see page 6). Roll to 13-inch circle ¼ inch thick.

2 Place crust on pizza pan; pinch edges for rim. Pour sauce on crust. Cut hot dogs into thin slices. Top pizza with hot dog, cheese, and relish.

Bake about 15 minutes

3 Bake at 425° till crust edges of pizza are golden brown, about 15 minutes. Top with green pepper rings. Cut into 8 pieces with pizza cutter.

Creamed beef on toast

You'll need:	Take out:
1 3- or 4-ounce package dried *or* smoked beef	kitchen shears
¼ cup butter or margarine	small bowl
¼ cup all-purpose flour	measuring cups
2 cups milk	saucepan
4 slices toast or 4 Baked Potatoes, split lengthwise (page 50)	wooden spoon

1 Use kitchen shears to snip beef into small pieces in small bowl. Set beef aside while you prepare the cream sauce.

2 Melt butter in saucepan. Blend in flour. Add milk all at once. Cook and stir till thick and bubbly. Stir in beef.

3 Cook till heated through, about 2 to 3 minutes. Pour some sauce over each piece of toast or potato. Serves 4.

Cheesy Bean Bake

You'll need: 2 tablespoons butter or margarine; 2 tablespoons all-purpose flour; ¼ teaspoon salt; 1 cup milk; two 16-ounce cans cut green beans, drained; 1 cup shredded process American cheese; ½ cup crushed saltine crackers.
Take out: saucepan, measuring spoons and cups, spoon, can opener, 1-quart casserole.

Set oven at 350°. Melt butter; blend in flour and salt. Add milk. Cook and stir till bubbly. Stir in beans and cheese. Pour in casserole. Top with crackers. Bake 20 to 25 minutes.

Creamed Peas on Potatoes

You'll need: one 10-ounce package frozen peas; ¼ cup butter or margarine; ¼ cup all-purpose flour; ½ teaspoon salt; 2 cups milk; 6 medium Baked Potatoes (page 50), split lengthwise.
Take out: 2 saucepans, measuring spoons, measuring cups, wooden spoon, potholder.

Cook peas following package directions; drain off liquid. Melt butter in saucepan. Blend in flour and salt. Add milk all at once. Cook and stir till thick and bubbly. Stir in peas. Heat through. Serve over potatoes.

Scalloped tuna

You'll need:	1 6½- or 7-ounce can tuna	About 30 single saltine crackers	6 tablespoons butter or mar- garine, melted	1 tablespoon chopped onion	Dash pepper	1 cup milk
Take out:	can opener, mixing bowls, fork, paper or plastic bag, rolling pin, measuring cups and spoons, paring knife, 9-inch pie pan, spoon, potholders					

1 Set oven at 400°. Open can of tuna; pour off liquid. Put tuna in bowl. Flake (break apart) tuna with a fork.

2 Crush saltine crackers in a bag with rolling pin. Do not crush too fine. Measure 1½ cups of cracker crumbs.

3 Combine crackers, butter, onion, and pepper in bowl. Put ⅓ mixture in buttered pie pan. Spoon in half the tuna.

4 Repeat layers of crumbs and tuna. Cover with last ⅓ crumbs. Pour milk over. Bake for 20 minutes. Serves 4.

Sauces for Scalloped Tuna

Choose one of these sauces to serve over the Scalloped Tuna.

Mushroom Sauce: Combine one 10½-ounce can condensed cream of mushroom soup and ⅓ cup milk in saucepan. Cook and stir with wooden spoon over medium heat until sauce is smooth and hot. Makes about 1½ cups.

Cheddar Cheese Sauce: Combine one 10¾-ounce can condensed Cheddar cheese soup and ⅓ cup milk in saucepan. Stir with a wooden spoon till well combined. Stir over medium heat until smooth and hot. Makes 1½ cups.

Fluffy scrambled eggs with Crispy bacon

Prepare the Crispy Bacon first so the Fluffy Scrambled Eggs will be piping hot when you serve them. Be careful not to overcook the eggs; they should be moist and glossy after cooking.

You'll need:	 6 eggs	⅓ cup milk	¾ teaspoon salt	Dash pepper	2 tablespoons butter	Bacon

Take out: mixing bowl, rotary eggbeater, measuring cup and spoons, skillets, pancake turner, metal tongs, paper toweling.

1 Break eggs into bowl. Beat fluffy with rotary egg-beater so no white shows. Stir in milk, salt, and pepper.

2 Melt butter in skillet. Pour in egg mixture. Cook gently over *low* heat. Turn with pancake turner. Cook 5-8 minutes.

Crispy Bacon

Bacon is easy to prepare when you cook it this way. Place the bacon slices in a *cold* skillet. Set the heat moderately *low*, and cook the bacon very slowly. Turn pieces with metal tongs. When bacon is done just the way you like it, remove it from skillet. Put bacon slices on paper toweling to drain off extra fat. Towels also help bacon stay hot until ready to serve.

Stuffed eggs

You'll need:	 6 eggs	2 tablespoons mayonnaise	1 teaspoon vinegar	1 teaspoon prepared mustard	½ teaspoon salt	Dash pepper	¼ teaspoon paprika

Take out:	covered saucepan, potholder, paring knife, small bowl, fork, measuring spoons, spoon, serving plate

1 Put eggs in pan. Cover with cold water. Heat to boiling. Cover; turn heat *very low*. Cook for 20 minutes.

2 Cool the eggs in cold water. Then, tap them lightly all over to make them crack. Peel under cold, running water.

3 Carefully cut the eggs in half lengthwise. Remove the yolks and put them in small bowl. Put whites aside till later.

4 Mash yolks. Stir in mayonnaise, vinegar, mustard, salt, pepper, and paprika till smooth. Spoon into whites.

Main Dish Ideas

Cheesy Luncheon Loaf

Set oven at 350°. Cut one 12-ounce can luncheon meat into 8 sections, cutting more than halfway through. *Do not cut through completely*. Spread *every other* cut with prepar-  ed mustard and pickle relish. Fold 4 slices process American cheese in half. Insert one cheese slice, folded side up, in the same 4 cuts with mustard and pickle relish. Bake till the cheese is lightly browned, about 20 minutes. To serve, slice loaf through unfilled cuts, making 4 pieces with cheese, mustard, and relish in the middle of each serving.

Polka Dot Soup

Pass a basket of crackers, breadsticks, or sliced French bread with steaming bowls of this colorful soup. With a knife, slice 3 hot dogs crosswise into thin circles. With can opener, open one 10½-ounce can condensed tomato soup. Pour the tomato soup into a saucepan. Fill the soup can with milk. Gradually pour milk into tomato soup in saucepan, stirring with a spoon till the mixture is smooth. Cook and stir over medium heat till mixture is hot, about 5 minutes. Add hot dog slices to tomato soup. Cook 2 to 3 minutes more. Pour soup into 4 soup bowls. Sprinkle with grated Parmesan cheese. Makes 4 servings.

Scrambled Eggs with Meat or Cheese

Select your favorite kind of luncheon meat and snip a slice into small pieces. Follow the directions for making Fluffy Scrambled Eggs on page 41, *except* add the luncheon meat pieces to the melted butter or margarine and brown the meat slightly before adding the egg mixture. When the eggs are done, you have your meat and eggs all in one dish. To make Scrambled Eggs with Cheese, simply add ¼ cup shredded cheese to the egg mixture *before* cooking. The cheese melts as you cook the eggs.

Make-Your-Own Pizza

Let your friends select their favorite toppers before the pizza bakes. Have a number of pepperoni slices, sliced olives, bacon bits, pickle relish, cheese, cut-up luncheon meat, and other foods that you and your friends like. Serve each topping in small dishes. Ask each friend to top his share of the frozen cheese pizza with his favorite toppings. Then, bake the pizza according to the label directions. To serve, cut the pizza with a pizza cutter. Then, ask each guest to 'identify' his pizza.

Pigs in Bacon

Set oven temperature at 425°. Allow 2 hot dogs apiece if you are really hungry. With a paring knife, cut a lengthwise slit in each hot dog. *Don't cut through completely*.  Spread some prepared mustard in each slit. Wrap a slice of bacon around each hot dog in a spiral. Fasten the ends of bacon by inserting wooden picks through each end of hot dog. Place a wire rack on a baking sheet. Lay wrapped hot dogs on rack. Bake in oven about 17 minutes. Turn at 'halftime' with metal tongs. Remove wooden picks before serving. Eat these with a fork and knife or in a hot-dog bun. Serve with crisp potato chips and cold milk.

Minute Steaks

The meatman runs this meat through a tenderizing machine so that it will be nice and tender to eat. Sometimes, minute steaks are also called cube steaks. Melt 1 tablespoon shortening in a skillet over moderate heat. Put in minute steaks with metal tongs or pancake turner. Cook 1 to 2 minutes on one side. Turn meat with metal tongs or pancake turner. Brown the other side 1 or 2 minutes more. Sprinkle the meat with salt and pepper. Serve at once. Baked Potatoes (page 50), buttered peas (place pat of butter atop peas before serving), and a Pretty Relish Tray (page 47) make a complete meal.

chapter 4

Salads and Vegetables

Molded fruit salad

You'll need:

1 3-ounce package
lime-flavored
gelatin

1 cup
boiling water

1 20-ounce
can pineapple
tidbits (2½ cups)

2 medium
bananas

Take out: loaf pan, measuring cup, spoon, can opener, bowl, sieve, paring knife

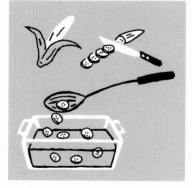

1 Put lime-flavored gelatin in loaf pan with 1 cup of boiling water. Stir to dissolve gelatin. Open can of pineapple.

2 Drain pineapple over measuring cup. Add water to juice to make 1 cup; stir into gelatin. Chill till partially set.

3 Peel bananas; slice crosswise into circles. Stir banana and pineapple into gelatin. Chill till firm.

Strawberry-pineapple freeze

You'll need:

1 10-ounce package
frozen straw-
berries, thawed
1 8¾-ounce can
crushed pineapple
1 cup strawberry-
flavored yogurt
¼ cup sifted pow-
dered sugar
3 pineapple rings
Lettuce

Take out:

bowl
fork
can opener
spoon
ice cube tray
foil
knife

Plan to serve Strawberry-Pineapple Freeze with Macaroni and Cheese (page 37). Because the salad is made ahead, you have more time to make the main dish for an easy dinner.

1 Put undrained strawber-
ries in bowl. Mash with a
fork. Open can of crushed
pineapple; drain off the liquid..
Stir drained pineapple, yogurt,
and sugar into berries.

2 Line ice cube tray with
foil, having foil extend 3
inches on each side. Pour in
fruit mixture; fold the foil
over fruit. Freeze till salad is
firm, about 3 hours.

3 Lift salad and foil from
tray; let stand a few minutes to soften. Cut salad into
6 wedges. Cut pineapple rings
in half; arrange atop each
wedge. Serve on lettuce.

Tuna salad

You'll need:	Take out:
2 eggs	saucepan
1 6½- or 7-	potholder
ounce can	knife
tuna, drained	bowl
and flaked	can opener
½ cup chopped	measuring
celery	cups
2 sweet	fruit juicer
pickles,	measuring
chopped	spoons
Dash salt	wooden spoon
1 tablespoon	
lemon juice	
⅓ cup	
mayonnaise	
Lettuce	

1 To hard-cook eggs, see Stuffed Eggs recipe on page 42. Cool eggs. Tap them to crack; peel under cold water. Cut up eggs in bowl.

2 Add tuna, celery, pickle, salt, and lemon juice. Stir in mayonnaise; toss. Chill. Line bowl with lettuce; spoon in salad.

Potato salad

You'll need:	Take out:
6 medium potatoes	2 covered
3 eggs	saucepans
1 cucumber, chopped	potholder
1 cup chopped celery	paring knife
2 tablespoons chopped	bowl
green onion	measuring cups
1½ teaspoons salt	measuring spoons
¼ cup French dressing	spoon
½ cup mayonnaise	

1 Scrub potatoes. Leave skins on. Cook, covered, in enough boiling, salted water to cover potatoes. Cook till a fork pricks easily, 25 to 40 minutes. Drain. Let cool.

2 To hard-cook eggs, see Stuffed Eggs recipe on page 42. Cool eggs; crack and peel under cold, running water. Peel potatoes. Cube potatoes and slice eggs into a bowl.

3 Add cucumber, celery, green onion, salt, French dressing, and mayonnaise to bowl. Toss ingredients lightly. Chill the salad at least 4 to 6 hours. Makes 6 to 8 servings.

Pretty relish tray

You'll need: Radishes   Green onions   Ice

Take out: paring knife, cutting board, bowl, serving bowl or plate

Before you cut: Wash the radishes. Cut off the tops of radishes with paring knife.

After you cut: Pop the radishes in bowl with ice water to open. Arrange them on a tray with the onions.

Roses: Start at end away from stem. With paring knife tip, mark 5 or 6 petals. Carefully cut thin petals.

Accordions: Cut radishes crosswise in about 10 to 12 narrow slices. *Don't cut completely through.*

Green onions: Wash onions under cold, running water. Trim off roots; cut off half the tops.

Tossed green salad

You'll need:

½ head lettuce
⅓ cup chopped celery
¼ cup sliced radishes
2 tablespoons sliced green onion
2 tomatoes
¼ cup French dressing

Take out:

salad bowl
paring knife
measuring cups
measuring spoons
salad fork and spoon

1 Tear bite-sized pieces of lettuce into large salad bowl. Use your fingers. Add celery, radishes, and onion.

2 Wash tomatoes under cold water. Carefully cut out the stem ends. Slice into wedges. Add to mixture in salad bowl.

3 Pour French dressing over the salad. Toss ingredients gently with a salad fork and spoon. Makes 4 servings.

Sunny carrots

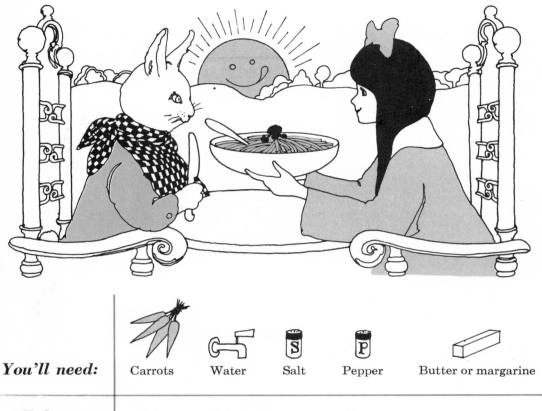

You'll need: Carrots Water Salt Pepper Butter or margarine

Take out: vegetable peeler, paring knife, covered saucepan, fork

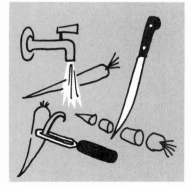

1 Wash carrots and peel with vegetable peeler. (Scrape away from you.) When carrots are peeled, use paring knife to cut them into 1-inch pieces.

2 Put 1 inch cold water in pan. Add salt till water tastes pleasantly salty. Bring water to a boil. Add carrots; cover. Cook 15 to 20 minutes.

3 Use a fork to test for tenderness. When carrots are tender, put them in a bowl. Season with salt and pepper. Add a pat of butter on top.

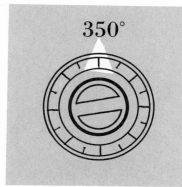

Scalloped corn

1 Set the oven temperature at 350°. This recipe will make 6 servings.

You'll need:

30 saltine crackers
1 16-ounce can cream-style corn
1 cup milk
1 beaten egg
2 tablespoons finely chopped onion
¼ teaspoon salt
Dash pepper
1 tablespoon butter

Take out:

plastic bag
rolling pin
can opener
measuring cups
8-inch round
   baking dish
spoon
measuring spoons
skillet
potholder

2 Put crackers in plastic bag. Coarsely crush with rolling pin to make 1½ cups.

3 Combine cream-style corn and milk in baking dish. Stir in egg. Add *1 cup* of the crushed crackers, chopped onion, salt, and pepper.

4 In a skillet melt the butter over *low* heat. Watch carefully so it does not burn. Combine remaining ½ cup cracker crumbs with butter.

5 Sprinkle butter and crumb mixture over top of the casserole. Bake at 350° for 30 to 35 minutes. Remove baking dish with potholder.

Baked potatoes

You'll need: Potatoes   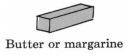 Butter or margarine

Take out: vegetable brush, fork, paper toweling, paring knife, potholder

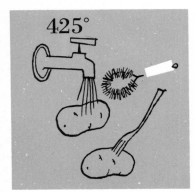

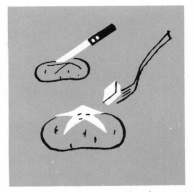

1 Set oven at 425°. Scrub dirt off potatoes. Stick with a fork to make holes for the hot steam to escape.

2 Put potatoes on oven rack. Bake potatoes 40 to 60 minutes. They will be soft when squeezed with toweling.

3 Cut a cross in the top of each potato with a paring knife. Place a pat of butter or margarine in each opening.

French-fried potatoes

You'll need: 1 package frozen French-fried potatoes   Salt

Take out: paper napkin, bowl or basket, shallow pan, potholder

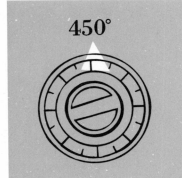

1 Set oven at 450°. Place a pretty paper napkin in a bowl or basket to put French fries in when they are done.

2 Spread frozen French-fried potatoes out in a shallow pan. Put in the oven; bake potatoes 15 to 20 minutes.

3 Remove pan from oven with potholder. Put potatoes in bowl or basket. Sprinkle with salt. Serve immediately.

Salad and Vegetable Ideas

Tomato Sandwich Salad

Serve this super salad in the summertime. Wash lettuce leaves; shake off water. Arrange lettuce leaves on salad plate. Wash tomato (use one that is well chilled); slice in thirds crosswise. Put the bottom tomato  slice on lettuce. Top with layer of some cottage cheese. Sprinkle with salt and pepper. Add another tomato slice, then more cottage cheese. Top with tomato slice and a sprig of parsley.

Peter Rabbit Salad

This is fun to serve at a birthday dinner or at Easter time. Wash and dry lettuce leaves. Put on salad plates. Place a canned pear half, round side up, in  the center of each plate. Use marshmallow quarters for the ears and a marshmallow half for the tail. The nose is a red maraschino cherry. Stick in whole cloves for the eyes.

VEGETABLE COOKERY

Canned Vegetables

These are already cooked, so all you do is heat them before serving. To heat, open can, pour liquid, but not vegetables, into a saucepan. Boil away part of the liquid in the saucepan. Add the vegetables and sprinkle with salt and pepper. And, if you wish, add a pat of butter. Heat till the vegetables are hot through. Serve.

Frozen Vegetables

Directions on the package will be your biggest help with these. The directions will tell you just how to prepare the food in 1-2-3 steps. Remember, don't thaw frozen vegetables before cooking. All frozen vegetables cook quickly.

Fresh Vegetables

Printed directions don't come with these, but here's what you want to remember:
1. Wash the vegetables thoroughly. Scrub them if they need it. You'll want the whole panful of vegetables to get done at the same time, so cut them into pieces about the same size.
2. How much water you'll need to use is the first thing to decide. Ask Mother to help you judge how much water you need. You don't want to float all the vitamins and minerals away, but neither do you want burned vegetables.
3. Add salt to the *cold* water so you can taste to tell when it's pleasantly salty (this takes about ½ teaspoon salt to 1 cup water).
4. Bring *water* to boiling.
5. *Now*, put in the vegetables; cover the pan.
6. Wait for a minute or so, and peek under the cover once in awhile. You start counting cooking time when the water starts to boil again.
7. Turn down heat so vegetables simmer gently. If the heat is too high, vegetables may boil over and cook dry before they're done. Vegetables are done when they're *just* tender. The table below gives you an idea of how long this will take. Either test with a fork or take a piece from the pan and, when cool, taste it.
8. Nobody likes cold vegetables unless they're supposed to be that way. Lift vegetables from pan with a slotted spoon and serve at once.

Vegetable cooking times

Asparagus	10 to 15 minutes
Beans, green or wax	15 to 30 minutes
Beets, whole	35 to 60 minutes
Broccoli	10 to 20 minutes
Brussels sprouts	10 to 15 minutes
Cabbage, shredded	5 to 7 minutes
wedges	10 to 12 minutes
Carrots, cut up	15 to 20 minutes
Cauliflower, flowerets	10 to 15 minutes
Corn on the cob	6 to 8 minutes
Peas, green	8 to 15 minutes
Potatoes, whole or halves	25 to 40 minutes
Spinach	3 to 5 minutes
Tomatoes, cut up	10 to 15 minutes
Turnips, sliced or cubed	15 to 20 minutes

chapter 5

Desserts

Nutty fudge sundae

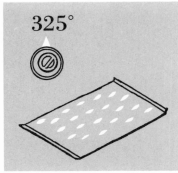

325°

1 Set oven at 325°. Arrange single layer of almonds on baking sheet. Bake till nuts are lightly toasted, about 15 minutes. Using potholder to remove pan from oven, stir nuts occasionally. Let cool.

2 Scoop big scoops of vanilla ice cream into serving dishes. Spoon fudge topping atop ice cream. Let it drizzle down the sides of the ice cream. Sprinkle some toasted almonds over the topping.

You'll need:	Take out:
	baking sheet potholder spoon ice cream scoop
Unblanched sliced almonds Vanilla ice cream Fudge topping	

Learn how easy it is to toast these golden, crunchy almonds in the oven to make a Nutty Fudge Sundae. Vanilla ice cream and creamy fudge topping complete the dessert.

Ice cream pops

You'll need:	Take out:
1 pint vanilla brick ice cream 4 wooden sticks 1 5-ounce bar milk chocolate ¼ cup shortening	sharp knife shallow pan double boiler measuring cup spoon table knife

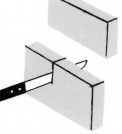 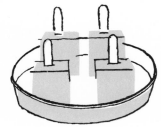  

1 Cut ice cream in two. Cut each piece again. Insert a stick in end of each.

2 Put pops in pan and freeze. Boil 2 inches water in bottom of double boiler.

3 Melt chocolate and shortening in the top of the double boiler; mix well.

4 Let chocolate and shortening cool till warm. Spread over pops. Freeze.

Yumsicles

You'll need:	1 package unsweetened flavored soft drink powder	4 cups water	¾ cup sugar
Take out:	pitcher, measuring cups, spoon, paper cups, wooden sticks		

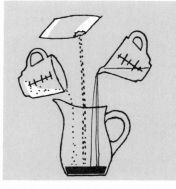  

1 Put soft drink powder in pitcher. Add water and sugar. Stir till dissolved.

2 Fill paper cups ¾ full with drink. Put in level part of freezer. Freeze till mushy.

3 When mushy, insert a wooden stick in each. Freeze solid. Tear off cups.

Baked apples

1 Set oven at 350°. Wash apples under cold, running water. Dry them. Carefully use corer to remove cores. Peel strip from top of each.

2 Put apples in a baking dish. Combine brown sugar and cinnamon. Fill apple centers with brown sugar mixture. Pour water around apples.

3 Put cover on baking dish. Bake about 60 minutes. Test doneness with a fork. If fork doesn't prick easily, put apples back in oven for baking.

Bake juicy apples with their centers packed full of a mixture of brown sugar and cinnamon. The sweet mixture melts as it bakes and becomes part of the golden sauce to be spooned over each apple. Pass a cold pitcher of cream to pour over Baked Apples.

You'll need:	*Take out:*
6 apples	apple corer
½ cup packed brown sugar	covered baking dish
	bowl
½ teaspoon ground cinnamon	measuring cups and spoons
	spoon
1 cup water	potholder
	fork

Chocolate mint cups

1 In bowl combine cereal, coconut, and nuts. Heat to boiling 2 inches water in bottom of double boiler; lower heat so water simmers. Melt chocolate in double boiler top.

You'll need:	1 cup slightly crushed crisp rice cereal, ⅓ cup flaked coconut, ¼ cup finely chopped walnuts, 1 cup semisweet chocolate pieces, 6 paper bake cups, peppermint ice cream
Take out:	bowl, measuring cups, double boiler, spoon, muffin pan, ice cream scoop

This is a different and fun-to-make dessert that you and your friends or family will enjoy eating. The cup is made with many things you like—rice cereal, coconut, nuts, and chocolate. A scoop of peppermint ice cream fills each Chocolate Mint Cup.

2 Pour chocolate into cereal; stir to coat. Line 6 muffin pans with paper bake cups. With spoon, press ⅓ cup mixture firmly onto bottom and sides of each cup to form shell.

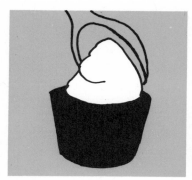

3 Put muffin pan in refrigerator to chill shells. Take out of refrigerator 15 minutes before filling. Remove paper cups. Fill each shell with a scoop of peppermint ice cream.

Date-marshmallow log

You'll need:	16 marshmallows, 1 cup pitted dates, 30 graham crackers, 2 cups chopped walnuts, 1 cup whipping cream
Take out:	kitchen shears, bowl, measuring cups, paper bag, rolling pin, waxed paper

1 Snip each marshmallow into 4 pieces. Wet shears between cuts to prevent sticking. Put marshmallows in bowl.

2 Snip dates with shears. Finely crush crackers in bag with rolling pin. Add dates, crackers, and nuts to bowl.

3 Stir in the whipping cream. *Note:* It is *not* whipped first. When cream is blended in thoroughly, turn mixture out on sheet of waxed paper.

4 Shape into a 3-inch roll. Wrap roll in waxed paper and chill in the refrigerator for several hours or overnight. Cut in 8 slices to serve.

Chocolate peppermint delicious

You'll need:	2 ounces peppermint stick candy, ½ of 8-ounce box chocolate wafers, 1 cup whipping cream
Take out:	paper or plastic bags, rolling pin, bowl, rotary eggbeater, spoon, ice cube tray

1 Put candy into bag. Roll with a rolling pin until crumbs form in the bag. This recipe makes 8 servings.

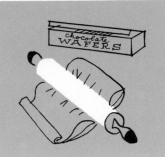

2 Put cookies into a second bag. Roll until thoroughly crushed. In chilled bowl, whip cream with rotary eggbeater.

3 Add candy and cookie crumbs to bowl. Mix gently. Turn into ice cube tray. Freeze till firm in the freezer.

Butterscotch pudding crunch

The next time you make dinner, make this creamy Butterscotch Pudding Crunch with crushed English toffee bars. It's so fast to make, and you can keep it in the refrigerator until serving time.

You'll need:	1 4-ounce package *instant* butterscotch pudding mix 4 chocolate-covered English toffee bars ¼ cup toasted flaked coconut
Take out:	bowls, rotary eggbeater, paper or plastic bag, rolling pin, measuring cup, spoon, 4 serving dishes

1 Read directions on the package of butterscotch pudding mix. Prepare as package directs for pudding. Let stand 5 to 10 minutes.

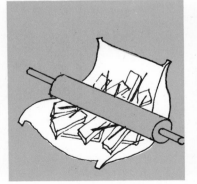

2 Put English toffee bars in paper or plastic bag, and crush bars thoroughly with rolling pin. Put crushed candy in bowl. Stir in coconut.

3 In 4 serving dishes spoon in *half* the pudding; sprinkle *half* the candy mixture in each. Add remaining pudding. Top with rest of candy.

Creamy lemon pie

You'll be proud to serve this mouth-watering pie at a family dinner or a fancy party. You can use other pie fillings in the delicate, graham-cracker piecrust.

Crumb crust

You'll need:	*Take out:*
11 graham crackers	paper or plastic bag
	rolling pin
	measuring cup and spoons
2 tablespoons sugar	small bowl
	small skillet
	spoon
5 tablespoons butter or margarine	8-inch pie pan

Save some of the crumb mixture to make a pretty design on top of Creamy Lemon Pie. The star design makes it easy to cut the pie in six even pieces, but you may want to make up your own design.

1 Put graham crackers in a bag. Crush with rolling pin. Measure 1 cup crumbs.

2 Put the 1 cup crumbs in a bowl; add sugar. Mix crumbs and sugar together.

3 Melt butter in skillet. Stir into crumb mixture; press in pie pan. Chill 45 minutes.

Lemon filling

You'll need:	1 egg	1 teaspoon grated lemon peel	3 lemons	1 14-ounce can sweetened condensed milk
Take out:	small bowl, fork, grater, waxed paper, measuring spoons and cup, knife, juicer, mixing bowl, spoon, can opener, rubber spatula			

1 Break 1 egg into small bowl. (Tap egg on side of bowl to crack it; pull shell apart with fingers.) Beat egg with fork till no white shows.

2 Grate lemon peel on waxed paper. Do not grate white part of lemon. (Be careful of fingers!) Measure 1 teaspoon of peel after you grate.

3 Now, cut the lemons in half. Squeeze in juicer till you have ½ cup lemon juice.

4 Pour milk in bowl. Add egg, peel, and juice. Stir *only* till thickened.

5 Spread lemon filling in the pie shell. Chill the pie for several hours, or till firm.

George Washington cherry pie

You'll need:

2 sticks
piecrust mix

Water

1 20-ounce can
cherry pie filling

Sugar

Take out: bowl, measuring cup, fork, rolling pin, 8-inch pie pan, can opener, knife, potholder

1 Set oven at 425°. Mix pastry following directions on package. Divide pastry in half. Form into two balls.

2 On *lightly* floured surface roll one pastry ball out with rolling pin. Roll from center to edge till ⅛ inch thick.

3 Fold pastry in half. Carefully lift and lay over the pie pan; unfold and ease gently into pan. *Do not stretch.*

4 Trim pastry even with rim of pan. Open can of cherry filling. Pour filling into pie pan. Spread it out evenly.

5 Roll out and fold second pastry ball. Place over pie. Trim ½ inch beyond edge. Tuck edges under; pinch together.

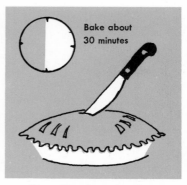

6 Cut slits in top of pastry for hot steam to escape. Sprinkle top with a little sugar; bake for about 30 minutes.

Boston cream pie

Boston Cream Pie is really a funny name for a dessert that is actually a cake. Whatever you want to call it, this dessert is filled with a luscious vanilla cream pudding between the yellow cake layers and is topped with a satiny chocolate glaze.

350°

You'll need:	Shortening All-purpose flour 1 2-layer-size yellow cake mix 1 package *instant* vanilla pudding mix 1 1-ounce square unsweetened chocolate 1 tablespoon butter or margarine 1 cup sifted powdered sugar ½ teaspoon vanilla 3 to 4 teaspoons water
Take out:	two 9 × 1½-inch round pans, bowls, electric mixer, rubber spatula, wire racks, rotary egg-beater, serving platter, spoon, small saucepan, measuring cup, measuring spoons, knife

1 Set oven at 350°. Prepare cake pans and mix following package directions. Cool and remove from pans.

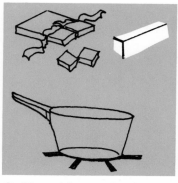

2 Prepare pudding mix following directions for pudding. Let stand 10 minutes. Lay 1 cake on platter, bottom side up. Spread pudding over.

3 Top with second cake, bottom side down. In pan, stir chocolate and butter over *low* heat till melted. Remove; stir in sugar and vanilla.

4 Blend enough water into chocolate mixture so it will pour easily. Spread chocolate mixture over top cake layer. Chill. Makes 8 servings.

Take Peanut Butter Cupcakes to school or to a picnic in your lunch box. The peanut butter flavor is in the crumb topping. A carton of cold milk will make them taste extra good.

Peanut butter cupcakes

You'll need:

¼ cup packed brown sugar
¼ cup sifted all-purpose flour
2 tablespoons peanut butter
1 tablespoon butter, melted
½ teaspoon ground cinnamon
⅓ cup shortening
½ cup granulated sugar
1 teaspoon vanilla
1 egg
1¼ cups sifted all-purpose flour
1½ teaspoons baking powder
¼ teaspoon salt
½ cup milk
12 paper bake cups

Take out:

2 bowls
measuring cups
measuring spoons
fork
spoon
flour sifter
electric mixer
rubber spatula
muffin pan
potholder

1 Set oven temperature at 375°. In a small bowl combine brown sugar, ¼ cup flour, peanut butter, butter, and ground cinnamon; stir till crumbly. Set mixture aside.

2 Put shortening, granulated sugar, and vanilla in bowl; beat with electric mixer till fluffy and creamy. Add egg; beat well. Sift together flour, baking powder, and salt.

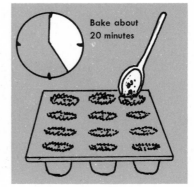

3 Add flour to creamed mixture alternately with milk. Beat well after each addition. Fill paper bake cups in muffin pans half full. Sprinkle topping over. Bake 20 minutes.

Dessert Ideas

Doughnut Sundaes

Before you start to assemble the sundaes, make *Hopscotch Butterscotch Sauce* like this: In a small saucepan mix together 3 tablespoons melted butter, ½ cup brown sugar, and ¼ cup light  cream. Simmer for 5 minutes. Beat ½ minute, and it's ready to use. To fix the sundaes, split doughnuts in half crosswise. Place each of the bottom halves on a separate dessert plate. Cover the bottom doughnut halves with spoonfuls of butter pecan ice cream. Then, press the doughnut 'lids' on the tops. Drizzle the sundaes with the Hopscotch Butterscotch Sauce.

Dress-Up Doughnuts

Use doughnuts from the bakery or supermarket for these glamorous snack or dessert ideas. One idea is to spread the rim of each doughnut with marshmallow creme and roll in chopped red maraschino cherries. Or, spread doughnuts with peanut butter and roll in chopped peanuts. Softened cream cheese and chopped pecans taste good together, too. Spread cream cheese on doughnuts; roll in chopped pecans.

Lacy Cake Topper

Instead of frosting a cake, place a fancy paper doily on top of the cake; sift powdered sugar lightly and evenly over the doily. Now, *carefully* lift off the doily. The lacy design of the sugar makes a pretty topping for special occasions.

Hot Chocolate-Peppermint Sundae

You can make this dessert in a hurry just before serving or when some unexpected guests drop by to see you. For a half cup of sauce you'll need 12 chocolate fondant-filled mint patties and 2 tablespoons light cream. Melt mints over water in top of double boiler (see page 69). Remove from heat and add cream. Stir. Spoon over scoops of vanilla ice cream.

Crunchy Peach Cobbler

Make this during the summer when fresh peaches are in season. Set oven at 375°. Peel, pit, and slice 6 fresh peaches. Mix peaches with 1 cup sugar and 2 tablespoons lemon juice. Turn into 8 × 8 × 2-inch baking dish. In a mixing bowl combine one 14-ounce package oatmeal muffin mix and ¼ teaspoon ground nutmeg. Using a pastry blender, cut in ½ cup softened butter till mixture is like coarse crumbs. Spoon over peaches. Bake for 40 to 45 minutes. Cut in squares. Serve warm or cool with ice cream.

Ice-Cream Sandwiches

You won't mind eating these yummy 'dessert sandwiches' with a spoon instead of your fingers. Cut a brick of peppermint ice cream into 4 slices. Sandwich each ice cream slice between 2 graham crackers. Let everyone pour on his own *Glossy Fudge Sauce*. To make the rich fudge sauce in a hurry: Mix together 1 cup instant cocoa powder, ⅓ cup boiling water, and 1 tablespoon butter. Use warm or cool.

Marshmallow Bun-Rabbits

In the springtime, place a parade of these treats around a party-time cake. First, bake a yellow or white cake, following the directions given on the cake  mix package. Frost with a white frosting mix. Or, if you wish, tint frosting yellow with a little yellow food coloring.

Then, make a 'bunny' favor for each of the guests you have invited to the party. You might make a few extras to place around the cake plate. Use a wooden pick to fasten two marshmallows together. Use a piece of a wooden pick to fasten on a marshmallow quarter for a tail. Cut the bunny ears from stiff pink construction paper. Poke ears into the top marshmallow. Then, *very carefully* paint the face on the Marshmallow Bun-Rabbit—dip a wooden pick in red food coloring and draw on the 'dot' eyes and a smiling mouth. Add yellow 'whiskers.'

chapter 6

Cookies
and
Candies

Easy chocolate chippers

You'll need:	Take out:
Shortening	baking sheet
1 package 2-layer-size	measuring cups
yellow cake mix	nut chopper
¼ cup butter or margarine,	bowl
softened	spoon
⅓ cup milk	teaspoon
1 egg	pancake turner
1 cup semisweet chocolate	wire rack
pieces	
½ cup chopped walnuts	

1 Set oven at 375°. Lightly grease baking sheet with shortening. Stir cake mix, butter, milk, and egg in bowl.

2 Stir in chocolate pieces and walnuts. Drop from teaspoon, about 2 inches apart, onto greased baking sheet.

3 Bake for about 12 minutes. Let stand a few seconds before removing with turner. Cool on wire rack.

Raisin-oatmeal cookies

Bake Raisin-Oatmeal Cookies on one of those long winter week-ends when it is more comfortable to stay inside. These are a favorite with Mother and Father, too, so make plenty.

You'll need:

1 cup sifted all-purpose flour	½ teaspoon baking soda	½ teaspoon salt	1 teaspoon ground cinnamon	½ cup shortening
½ cup packed brown sugar	¼ cup granulated sugar	1 egg 2 tablespoons milk	2 cups quick-cooking rolled oats	1 cup raisins

Take out:

baking sheet, flour sifter, measuring cups and spoons, waxed paper, bowls, spatula, wooden spoon, pancake turner, wire rack

375°

1 Set oven at 375°. Lightly grease baking sheet with some shortening. Measure flour onto waxed paper. Add baking soda, salt, and cinnamon; sift ingredients into a bowl.

2 Add shortening, brown sugar, granulated sugar, egg, and milk; mix well. Beat mixture hard, about 100 times.

3 Add oats and raisins. Drop teaspoons of cookie mixture, 2 inches apart, onto the greased baking sheet.

Bake about 12 minutes

4 Bake 12 to 15 minutes. Remove cookies from sheet with a turner. Place on wire rack to cool. Store in jar.

Sugar drops

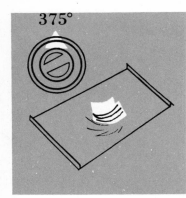

1 Set oven at 375°. Put a bit of shortening on waxed paper. Rub it over the baking sheets till lightly greased.

2 In a bowl soften shortening with back of wooden spoon. Mix sugar in thoroughly. Add egg; beat until fluffy. Add vanilla; mix in well.

You'll need:

⅔ cup shortening   ¾ cup sugar   1 egg   1 teaspoon vanilla

1½ cups sifted all-purpose flour   1½ teaspoons baking powder   ¼ teaspoon salt

4 teaspoons milk   ½ cup chopped walnuts   ½ cup raisins

Take out: waxed paper, baking sheets, measuring cups and spoons, bowl, wooden spoon, flour sifter, pancake turner, potholder, wire rack

3 Sift flour; measure. Then, sift again with baking powder and salt onto waxed paper. Set flour mixture aside.

4 Add milk to shortening mixture. Add flour mixture, nuts, and raisins. Mix. Drop by teaspoons on sheet.

Bake about 12 minutes

5 Bake about 12 minutes. Remove. Sprinkle on some sugar. While the first pan of cookies bakes, fix the next.

Picnic
some-mores

Try Picnic Some-Mores on picnics or inside the house. You can roast the marshmallows just as easily by the fireplace.

You'll need:	Take out:
\nMarshmallows	long-handled fork, skewer, or stick
Graham crackers	plates
Flat bars of milk chocolate	

1 Toast 2 marshmallows at a time on a long-handled fork or a long stick slowly so marshmallows will be hot and gooey inside.

2 Top 1 graham cracker with chocolate. Push the marshmallows onto the chocolate, then top with a cracker 'lid.'

Fudge brownies

You'll need:

1 package
brownie mix

½ cup
chopped walnuts

Canned chocolate
frosting

Sifted
powdered sugar

Take out: bowl, spoon, measuring cups, rubber spatula, baking pan, potholder, wire rack, can opener, knife, flour sifter

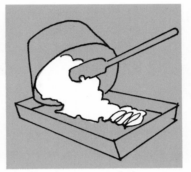

1 Set oven as package directs. Prepare brownie mix, following the directions on the package. Stir in chopped nuts.

2 Use the size of baking pan suggested on package. Turn mixture into pan. Bake as directed. Cool on rack.

3 Spread brownies with canned frosting; cut into squares. Top with walnut half. Or, dust with powdered sugar.

Dust sifted powdered sugar on the tops of some of the Fudge Brownies instead of spreading with creamy frosting. You will enjoy the sweet, melt-in-your-mouth flavor the sugar adds, and the family will like having two choices.

1 Heat 2 inches of water in bottom of double boiler. Grease baking pan with a bit of shortening on waxed paper.

2 Melt marshmallows, butter, and butterscotch in top of double boiler over water. Remove from heat; mix well.

3 Stir in cereal, walnuts, vanilla, and salt. Spread the mixture evenly in greased pan. Cut into 36 pieces.

Yummy butterscotch squares

You'll need:	Take out:
Shortening	double boiler
1 pound marshmallows	8-inch square
3 tablespoons butter	baking pan
8 ounces butterscotch	waxed paper
pieces	measuring spoons
1 cup crisp rice cereal	measuring cups
1 cup broken walnuts	wooden spoon
1 teaspoon vanilla	rubber spatula
½ teaspoon salt	potholder

Caramel nut balls

You'll need:	1 cup chopped nuts Butter ½ pound vanilla caramels 2 tablespoons hot water 16 marshmallows
Take out:	measuring cup, shallow pan, waxed paper, plate, double boiler, measuring spoons, wooden spoon, skewer, potholder

1 Spread nuts out in shallow pan. Lightly grease plate with bit of butter on a piece of waxed paper. Boil water in bottom of double boiler.

2 Put caramels and 2 tablespoons hot water in top of double boiler. Place over hot water in double boiler bottom. Stir to melt caramels.

3 Spear marshmallow with skewer. Dip into hot caramel sauce, then in nuts. Place on plate; repeat with remaining marshmallows.

1 Butter square pan lightly, using waxed paper. Sift and measure powdered sugar. Melt ½ cup butter in pan.

2 Stir in brown sugar. Cook and stir over low heat for 2 minutes. Stir in the milk. Cook till mixture is boiling.

3 Cool to room temperature. Beat in powdered sugar till like fudge. Stir in nuts; pour in pan. Chill and cut.

Quick
walnut penuche

You'll need:	Take out:
Butter	waxed paper
1¾ cups to 2 cups powdered sugar	8 × 8 × 2-inch pan
	flour sifter
½ cup butter or margarine	measuring cups
	1½-quart saucepan
1 cup packed brown sugar	wooden spoon
	potholder
¼ cup milk	rubber spatula
1 cup chopped walnuts	

Quick Walnut Penuche is really a light-colored fudge candy. The rich flavor comes from golden brown sugar and chewy walnuts. Store extra penuche in the refrigerator and surprise your friends with your own homemade candy.

Creamy fudge

You'll need:	Butter	1 6-ounce package semisweet chocolate pieces (1 cup)	2 3-ounce packages cream cheese	4 cups sifted powdered sugar	Dash salt	1 teaspoon vanilla	½ cup chopped walnuts

Take out:	waxed paper, 8 × 8 × 2-inch pan, double boiler, mixing bowl, wooden spoon, measuring cups and spoons, rubber spatula, knife

1 Lightly butter square pan. Put 2 inches water in the bottom of double boiler. Bring water to boiling.

2 Melt chocolate pieces in top of double boiler. Have the cream cheese at room temperature. Put cream cheese in a bowl.

3 Use wooden spoon to break up the cream cheese. Rub cheese against the bowl to soften; beat cheese until it is smooth.

4 Gradually stir in *half* of the sifted powdered sugar, salt, and the vanilla. Stir the mixture carefully.

5 Using a rubber spatula, pour melted chocolate into cheese mixture. Mix well. Add remaining sugar and nuts.

6 Press mixture into square pan. Chill in refrigerator till it is firm. Cut in squares. Top each piece with nut half, if you wish.

Crispy popcorn

You'll need:	Cooking oil	Popcorn	Salt
Take out:	electric popcorn popper, measuring spoons and cup, potholder, large bowl		

1 Have Mother show you how to use the popper. Heat 3 tablespoons oil in popper. Add ½ cup popcorn.

2 Put lid on popper. Listen for popcorn to stop popping before turning off heat. Use potholder to remove lid.

3 Carefully empty popcorn into large bowl. Sprinkle lightly with salt. Popcorn tastes best served hot.

Caramel apples

You'll need:	1 14-ounce package vanilla caramels 2 tablespoons water Dash salt Wooden skewers 4 or 5 apples
Take out:	measuring spoons, double boiler, baking sheet, waxed paper

1 Heat 2 inches water in double boiler bottom. Add caramels and water to top; stir till smooth. Add dash salt.

2 Stick skewers in stem end of apples; dip in caramel syrup and turn to coat. Add water if syrup thickens.

3 Set caramel apples on baking sheet covered with waxed paper. Chill till coating is firm. Serves 4 or 5.

Cookie and Candy Ideas

Perky Cookie Faces

These make good party-time favors. The cookie faces start out as vanilla wafers that you buy in a box at the supermarket. Simply sandwich 2 vanilla wa-fers with **Powdered Sugar Icing:** Mix ½ cup sifted powdered sugar with enough milk to make icing spread nicely. Using a salted peanut half as a 'topknot,' stick in icing. Ice front of cookie sandwich, and add semisweet chocolate pieces for the eyes.

Eat-Right-Away Cookies

No one will expect you to save any of these cookies for tomorrow. Mix 2 tablespoons honey and ½ cup coconut in bowl. Spread on 12 saltine crackers. Put on baking sheet and bake at 375° for about 7 minutes. Take them from the oven when they're golden brown. Then, serve while they are still toasty and warm.

Easy-To-Fix Cookies

Refrigerated cookie dough available at the supermarket gives cookie jar fillers a flying start. Choose from butterscotch, chocolate, oatmeal, and any other type of cookie that you like. Or, make two or three kinds to please everyone. Delicious cookies come from cookie mixes in boxes, too. Just follow the directions and bake the simple way suggested.

Coconut Snowballs

First, roll marshmallows in slightly beaten egg white. While they are still moist, roll them in fluffy coconut. Let the egg white-coconut mixture become firm.

Glitter Sugar Mallows

Dip big, fluffy marshmallows in a bowl of light cream. Then, roll them in pieces of glittering colored sugar. This candy is especially nice for garnishing plates of Christmas candies.

Chocolate Clouds

Melt a package of semisweet chocolate pieces in the top of the double boiler. Melt this the same way you melted choc-olate for Creamy Fudge (page 71). Dip the marshmallows to coat with chocolate; roll them in chopped nuts. Place Chocolate Clouds on a plate until the chocolate is cool and firm, then serve.

Stuffed Dates

You'll need 1 tablespoon butter or margarine, 1¾ cups sifted powdered sugar, 2 tablespoons orange juice, and one 6½-ounce package pitted dates. Soften butter with a spoon in a bowl. Sift and measure sugar. Add to butter in bowl. Beat well. Stir in orange juice.

Make pencil-like rolls out of the candy mixture. Cut short lengths of the candy rolls and stuff into each pitted date. Glistening jelly string gumdrops of different colors make a pretty trim for the Stuffed Dates. Adding a big walnut half to each one is a good idea, too.

Caramel Snappers:

For each piece you'll need 4 pecan halves, 1 vanilla caramel, and some semisweet choc-olate pieces. Arrange pecans and caramels on a buttered baking sheet as shown in the drawing. Heat at 325° for 4 to 8 minutes to soften the caramels. Remove from the oven. Mash softened caramels over pecans with a buttered fork. Let cool. While they are cooling, melt the chocolate pieces in top of a double boiler. Melt this the same way you melted chocolate for Creamy Fudge (page 71). When the caramels have cooled, spoon some melted chocolate over each candy. Let cool.

chapter 7

Meal Plans

Sunday breakfast

Let your parents be the lazybones and you be the early bird some Sunday morning. Set the table the night before. In the morning, round up all the ingredients and cooking utensils you are going to use. (You should check the ingredients you'll need before Mother goes shopping on Saturday so you will be sure to have everything. It is fun to go shopping with her and pick out the ingredients—with Mother's assistance, of course.)

First, decide what jobs you can have done before starting to cook. Use a small tray to place the juice glasses on. Pour the orange juice into glasses, and set the tray in the refrigerator so the orange juice will get icy cold.

Gather together all the good things that you are going to serve with French toast. Sift the powdered sugar so it will be nice and fluffy and not have any lumps, or serve it in a big shaker. Set the jelly and butter on the table. If you have time, the family will thank you for warming the syrup. All you do is heat the syrup in a saucepan over low heat. Serve the warm syrup in a heat-proof pitcher.

Make the cocoa and keep it warm. Cook the bacon next, and drain it on paper toweling. Cover it with more paper toweling to keep it warm until you are ready to serve. Set the orange juice on the table.

Call your parents as you begin to make the French toast. As they arrive at the table, offer them a cup of cocoa to sip as they chat with you and wait for the main course.

While the French toast gets brown and beautiful, set the crispy bacon on the table.

Who do you suppose enjoyed breakfast the most? Don't be surprised if Mother and Father (as well as the rest of the family) ask for another breakfast like this one soon.

Lightning lunch

```
┌─────────────────────────────────┐
│            MENU                  │
│                                  │
│   Polka-Dot Soup (page 43)       │
│ Peanut Butter-Honey Sandwiches   │
│     Shoestring Potatoes          │
│       Shiny Red Apples           │
│ Raisin-Oatmeal Cookies (page 65) │
└─────────────────────────────────┘
```

Family supper

```
┌─────────────────────────────────┐
│            MENU                  │
│                                  │
│    Bar-B-Q Burgers (page 19)     │
│ French-Fried Potatoes (page 50)  │
│  Tossed Green Salad (page 47)    │
│ Butterscotch Pudding Crunch      │
│          (page 57)               │
│            Milk                  │
└─────────────────────────────────┘
```

When the situation calls for a quick feast, you are just the cook to whip it up. And nothing dull about it, either. All you have to do is slice hot dogs into a canned soup and heat them together to make one delicious hot dish.

While the soup is heating, you make the peanut butter and honey sandwiches. For each sandwich, spread butter and peanut butter on one slice of bread. Put honey on the second slice of bread and then 'sandwich' them together. The crunchy potato sticks simply spill out of the can into a serving dish.

For the dessert, reach into the cookie jar, which is never empty—not the way you like to make and munch crisp cookies. Put the shiny red apples in a bowl, the cookies on a plate— to save yourself time in the kitchen later. Serve everyone a big glass of chilled milk.

This lunch is a good one for the lunch box, too. Pour the hot soup into a vacuum bottle, and wrap sandwiches, potatoes, and cookies.

Another quick lunch box idea is to begin with giant Lunch Box Heroes (page 21). Make sure you wrap the sandwiches snugly in plenty of plastic wrap. Wrap the lettuce separately so it will stay crisp. Then, put it in your sandwich when you're ready to eat. Select your favorite canned soup to heat up and pour into the vacuum bottle. A small bag of potato chips packs nicely in your lunch box. For your lunch box dessert, plan to make Peanut Butter Cupcakes (page 62) ahead of time, and pack them along with a fresh banana.

All your pals will want to trade their lunches for yours—especially when you tell them you made it yourself.

Saturday nights rate something special, but especially easy. And here it is. Maybe you'll like to have everyone come out to the kitchen to help himself—kind of a kitchen picnic.

Make the dessert well ahead of time so it can chill in the refrigerator. Have napkins, plates, silverware, a bowl of crisp, cool salad, a basket of fresh, hot French fries, and glasses of milk lined up neatly on the kitchen counter.

Let everyone pick up a big, soft, buttered bun and fix his own Bar-B-Q Burger. The makin's are bubbling in the skillet on the range. Use the same spoon you've been stirring with. Look out—you'll be getting orders for these every Saturday night at your house!

If you have a brother or sister who wants to act as assistant cook, here is another idea. Assign the dessert detail to your assistant, or make it ahead of time. Fill the cookie jar with Sugar Drops (page 66) the day before, and help your assistant gather the ingredients together for Baked Apples (page 54). If you want to serve the apples hot with lots of cream, let your assistant get them ready while you are making sandwiches and vegetable. Then, you can pop the apples into the oven while you are eating and serve them piping hot. Or, bake the apples and let them chill in the refrigerator till serving time. They are just as delicious cold.

The rest of the meal you can get ready in about 30 minutes before you plan to call supper. Clean the carrots and cut into chunks for Sunny Carrots (page 48) before you get too busy. The Egg in a Bun Sandwiches (page 22) are made with hamburger buns. These will taste good with tall glasses of cold milk.

76

Outdoor tea party

MENU

Tea-Party Sandwiches (*page 31*)
Easy Chocolate Chippers (*page 64*)
Frosty Lime Float (*page 11*)

Spread a blanket under a big shade tree in your backyard or set the lawn chairs up on the patio to treat some of your best friends to a mid-afternoon tea party. You can write the invitations on pretty paper tea napkins.

A tea party is an easy and simple snack served in the middle of the afternoon. Because you want to spend the time with your friends, everything is made ahead and put on the plates. Pour the refreshing floats last.

Picnic in the backyard

MENU

Hot Dogs (*page 18*)
Catsup and Mustard
Potato Salad (*page 46*)
Sliced Tomatoes   Crisp Pickles
Ice Cream Pops (*page 53*)
Circus Time Lemonade (*page 15*)

Everyone likes this kind of food on a picnic—steaming hot dogs, potato salad, ice cream—you just can't miss. But, of course, you want to show a little originality, and that's where the Ice Cream Pops come in. You make them in the morning and let them freeze hard in the freezer. Each one has its own wooden handle for easy eating—even outdoors. If you wish, you can letter a name on each handle.

A picnic isn't supposed to be a lot of trouble, so take advantage of all the shortcuts you can use. Use frozen lemonade and skip the lemon squeezing. You won't even have to figure out how much sugar to use. Have plenty of ice to make the lemonade chilly cold.

Count on paper plates, cups, and napkins for your outdoor feast. They come in all kinds of pretty colors and patterns. Save dishwashing!

Outdoor cookout

MENU

Hamburgers (*page 19*)
Pretty Relish Tray (*page 47*)
Potato Chips
Picnic Some-Mores (*page 67*)
Tutti-Frutti Ice Sparkle (*page 12*)

This is a great time to ask Father to help you cook. You can watch him build the fire and learn special 'safety hints' from him. Shape the hamburgers, following the recipe, then cook about 4 to 6 inches from the hot coals for about 5 minutes on each side. Turn hamburgers with a special long-handled pancake turner.

Make the crisp relishes ahead of time. Put the potato chips in a big bowl. Keep the sparkly beverage chilled in the refrigerator till serving time. Everyone joins in the fun and makes his own dessert over glowing coals.

Table setting

The good food you cook will look even better when it is served in an attractive way. Another important reason for proper table setting is that it makes eating more convenient.

1 The flatware (utensils for eating) and plate go 1 inch from the edge of the table.

2 If Father serves at your house, plates belong in a stack at his place.

3 Arrange flatware in the order you use it, from the outside in. The knives and spoons are on the right and forks on the left.

4 The knife blade turns toward the plate because that way it's ready to pick up.

5 The cup and saucer (beside the spoon, as you see in the drawing) and the glass for milk or water (at the tip of the knife) belong on the right side because most people pick them up with their right hand.

6 If you have a salad plate, it is placed on the left side by the fork. If you don't have a salad plate, the napkin goes beside the fork with the fold away from the plate. If table looks crowded, put napkin on dinner plate.

7 A decorative centerpiece helps brighten the table. Arrange a small bouquet of flowers or a bowl of fresh fruits.

Table manners

Mealtime should be a happy time for all. You can talk about what happened in school or at play today, as well as listen to what Mother and Father did. Mealtime is really a sociable event in which you learn many things that will make you comfortable and confident when eating away from home. It will also help put you at ease when you entertain at home. You will even discover that eating is more enjoyable when you are polite and considerate of others.

1 Wait until the whole family is seated before you begin eating. You may even want to help seat a special guest when you have one.

2 Contribute to the table conversation. Say 'Excuse me' if you must interrupt when someone else is talking or telling a story.

3 Talk about pleasant subjects. Maybe you could tell about the new girl or boy at school or how the baseball team did.

4 Be interested in what everyone has to say, and they will be interested in what you say.

5 Say 'Please' and 'Thank you' when you want something to be passed to you. Do not reach in front of other people.

6 Use both hands to pass food to the next person. Pass potholders with hot foods.

7 Keep your arms and elbows in your lap while eating; don't rest them on the table.

8 Cut food into small bite-sized pieces before eating. Break bread into pieces and butter each piece before you eat it.

9 Place knife and fork across the top of your plate when you are finished eating. Avoid resting them on the edge of your plate because they could fall off easily.

10 Blot your lips with your napkin as you eat. Fold your napkin neatly and place it beside your plate after eating.

11 Wait for the family to finish eating before excusing yourself from the table. Mother likes to hear a 'Thank you' for the meal.

Weights and measures

3 teaspoons = 1 tablespoon
4 tablespoons = ¼ cup
8 tablespoons = ½ cup
16 tablespoons = 1 cup
1 cup = 8 ounces
1 cup = ½ pint
2 cups = 1 pint
4 cups = 1 quart
4 quarts = 1 gallon

Sizes of cans

8 ounce = 1 cup
14 to 16 ounce = 1¾ cups
16 to 17 ounce = 2 cups
20 ounce (18 fluid ounces) = 2½ cups
29 ounce = 3½ cups

How much and how many

2 tablespoons butter = 1 ounce
1 stick or ¼ pound butter = ½ cup
1 square chocolate = 1 ounce
28 saltine crackers = 1 cup fine crumbs
14 square graham crackers = 1 cup fine crumbs
22 vanilla wafers = 1 cup fine crumbs
1½ slices bread = 1 cup soft crumbs
1 slice bread = ¼ cup fine dry crumbs
4 ounces macaroni (1–1¼ cups) = 2¼ cups cooked
4 ounces noodles (1½–2 cups) = 2 cups cooked
7 ounces spaghetti = 4 cups cooked
1 cup long grain rice = 3–4 cups cooked
1 cup packaged precooked rice = 2 cups cooked
Juice of 1 lemon = 3 tablespoons
Grated peel of 1 lemon = 1 teaspoon
Juice of 1 orange = about ⅓ cup
Grated peel of 1 orange = about 2 teaspoons
1 medium apple, chopped = about 1 cup
1 medium banana, mashed = about ⅓ cup
1 medium onion, chopped = about ½ cup
1 cup whipping cream = 2 cups whipped
1 pound American cheese, shredded = 4 cups
¼ pound blue cheese, crumbled = 1 cup
12 to 14 egg yolks = 1 cup
8 to 10 egg whites = 1 cup
1 pound walnuts in shell = 1½ to 1¾ cups shelled
1 pound almonds in shell = ¾ to 1 cup shelled

INDEX

THE GREAT WHITE SHARK

BY
CARL R. GREEN
WILLIAM R. SANFORD

EDITED BY
DR. HOWARD SCHROEDER
Professor in Reading and Language Arts
Dept. of Elementary Education
Mankato State University

PRODUCED AND DESIGNED BY
BAKER STREET PRODUCTIONS
Mankato, MN

CRESTWOOD HOUSE
Mankato, Minnesota

CIP

LIBRARY OF CONGRESS CATALOGING IN PUBLICATION DATA

Sanford, William R. (William Reynolds).
  The great white shark.

  SUMMARY: Examines the physical characteristics, habitat, life cycle, and behavior of this large and dangerous shark.
  1. White shark--Juvenile literature. (1. White shark. 2. Sharks) I. Green, Carl R. II. Title.
  QL638.95.L3S26   1985   597'.31   85-14936
  ISBN 0-89686-281-X (lib. bdg.)

International Standard Book Number:	Library of Congress Catalog Card Number:
Library Binding 0-89686-281-X	85-14936

ILLUSTRATION CREDITS:

Carl Roessler/Tom Stack & Assoc.: Cover, 22, 35, 42
Charles Nicklin/Ocean Images: 5, 17
Marcel Meyer/Tom Stack & Assoc.: 7
Ron & Valerie Taylor/Tom Stack & Assoc.: 8, 29, 37
Al Giddings/Ocean Images: 11, 15, 18, 21, 26, 32, 45
Bob Williams: 12, 30
Rick Mula/Ocean Images: 24-25
Valerie Taylor/Tom Stack & Assoc.: 38

CRESTWOOD HOUSE

Hwy. 66 South, Box 3427
Mankato, MN 56002-3427

TABLE OF CONTENTS

INTRODUCTION:

The waves rose high and blue-green under the early morning sky. Just beyond the surf line, several brown pelicans dived into the water to feed. On one end of the bay, sea lions sunned themselves on the rocks.

As far as Todd Harris could see, it was a perfect day. He carefully waxed his surfboard. The sea breeze felt cool, so he pulled on his wet suit. The other guys were in school and Todd had the beach to himself. The thought made him smile.

Todd carried his white surfboard into the foamy surf. He lay on the board and stroked hard. The sharp point bit into the water and slid forward. At the breaker line, Todd held tightly to the board and rolled under a crashing wave. He kicked twice, and broke through into calm water. His nerves tingled as the cold saltwater ran down his face.

Not far away, a long, graceful shadow moved along the bottom of the ocean. Smaller fish moved out of the way as the great white shark glided past.

As always, the great white shark was hungry. Suddenly, the line of fluid-filled canals that ran down its spine picked up a new vibration in the water. The signal sent to the shark's small brain was simple: "Food!"

Todd sat on his surfboard, his legs dangling down into the water. He was waiting for the perfect wave.

4

Below him, the great white shark eyed its prey. The black shape of the surfboard looked like a floating sea lion. With one sweep of its tail, the shark

A great white shark moves just below the surface of the ocean.

hurled itself upward. The huge mouth opened, showing rows of razor-sharp teeth.

On the surface, Todd finally saw the wave he wanted. Swiftly, he pulled his legs up into a kneeling position. At that moment something moving like a runaway train struck his surfboard. Todd heard only a weird crunching sound. As he tumbled into the water, he saw a long, grey-white body twisting away from him.

"Jaws!" was all Todd could think of; he swam hard and caught a wave that took him in to the beach. Behind him, the great white shark circled. It struck the surfboard again. The fiberglass didn't smell or taste like food. Finally, the shark swam away to find better prey.

Up on the beach, Todd said a prayer of thanks. A wave soon washed his surfboard up on the sand. Todd ran his fingers over the half-circle that the shark had bitten out of the edge of the surfboard. That could have been his leg!

When Todd stopped shaking, he went to the lifeguard station. The lifeguards thanked him for coming. Because great white shark attacks often are repeated, they put out a warning to all swimmers in the area.

Todd had laughed at the movie *Jaws* when he first saw it. Now he wasn't laughing. After his close call, he headed for the library. He wanted to find out more about the great white shark.

The "business end" of a fourteen-foot great white shark!

CHAPTER ONE:

The ancestors of today's sharks first appeared in the sea thousands of years ago. They were the first animals to develop teeth. Through the years, however, sharks haven't changed much. These fierce predators may be primitive, but they are very good at what they do!

Sharks were the first animals to develop teeth.

Sharks don't have bones

Like their early ancestors, today's sharks don't have a single bone in their bodies. Instead, a shark's skeleton is made of cartilage. This is the same tough, flexible material that gives shape to a human's nose. Most fish have skeletons made of bone.

Sharks differ from fish with bony skeletons in other ways, as well. Bony fish have a single gill opening on each side of their heads. By contrast, sharks have five to seven openings, called gill slits. In addition, most bony fish lay eggs that hatch outside the female's body. Shark pups, however, are usually born alive.

Bony fish have a swim bladder to help them float, but sharks lack this useful organ. As a result, a shark sinks when it stops swimming. Sharks can't swim backwards, either. Even the shark's skin is different. Instead of smooth scales, shark skin is rough and feels like sandpaper.

A large and dangerous family

More than three hundred different types of sharks live in the world's oceans. The largest shark that ever lived was the *Carcharodon megalodon.* This great predator was over fifty feet (15 m) in length. *Megalodon* is extinct, but a close relative still cruises the world's oceans — *Carcharodon carcharias.* The name is a good one, for it means "shark with sharp, jagged teeth." Better known as the great white shark, *carcharias* is the killer that scared everyone in the movie, *Jaws.*

Sharks vary in size from the six-inch (15 cm) midwater shark to the forty-foot (12 m) whale shark. The gentle whale shark, however, lives only on plankton. That leaves the great white as the shark world's biggest predator. The largest great white ever caught was twenty-one feet (6.4 m) long and weighed over four thousand pounds (1,815 kg). An average great white grows to fourteen feet (4.3 m), and weighs about three thousand pounds (1,360 kg).

Many sharks attack people, and the great white shark is the deadliest hunter of all. Marine biologists point out, however, that great whites don't go out of their way to eat people. A shark that attacks a swimmer is just looking for food.

Sharp teeth everywhere

The great white shark's rough skin is not pure white. The color varies from light gray to slate-brown to blue-black. The darker colors appear on

Great whites have dark backs and white bellies.

the shark's back, and fade to white on the belly. Under a microscope, you can see that the skin is covered with a type of scale called a denticle. Denticles look like small, sharp teeth. Swimmers who have scraped against these "teeth" have often lost a patch of their own skin!

The great white shark's strong jaws are lined from front to back with rows of large teeth. The teeth are three inches (7.6 cm) long and razor sharp. The great white's teeth are the largest of all the sharks! Each triangle-shaped tooth has saw-tooth edges, much like a steak knife. When the shark bites down, the jaws close with several tons of pressure. The great white can — and has — bitten off an elephant's leg!

Marine biologists sometimes call the great white shark a "tooth factory." Like other sharks, its teeth are not set in sockets in the jaw. Held in by tissue, the teeth fall out easily. Rows of new teeth are always ready to move into place, however. Over a lifetime, a great white will replace thousands of teeth.

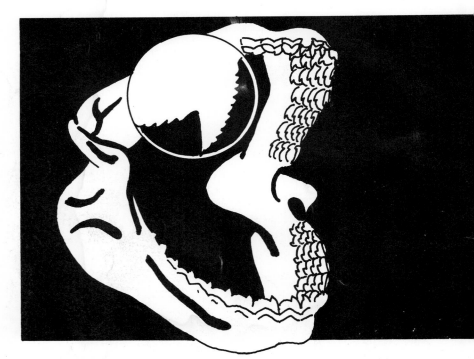

Thousands of saw-toothed edged teeth are replaced during the life of a shark.

A great white shark can bite a thirty-pound (13.6 kg) chunk out of its prey. Each mouthful is swallowed whole. If the shark swallows something it can't digest, it can spit it out. Even so, a great white taken from the Adriatic Sea had three overcoats and a license plate in its stomach! No one knows how they got there.

Once the shark has eaten, its strong stomach acids can make quick use of the food. The great white can also keep food in its stomach for several weeks before digesting it. By delaying digestion, the shark has food ready if it can't find fresh prey.

Keen senses for hunting

The great white shark finds its prey by sight, sound, and smell. Each of these senses works well in the shark's ocean habitat.

The large black eyes of a great white shark are good at spotting moving objects. The shark also sees well in the dim light deep below the ocean's surface. When the shark closes in on its prey, it depends on its eyesight to guide it to its target. Beyond fifty feet (15 m), however, the great white depends on sound and smell.

To find prey at a distance, the great white uses three separate "hearing" systems. Its ears can pick up very faint sounds. These sounds include high and low tones that humans can't hear. Sharks also "hear" with a sensitive system of fluid-filled canals. These canals run along the shark's back from its head to its tail. The canals detect both motion and sound through changes in water pressure. Great whites have a third "hearing" system located in their snouts. A series of sensory pores in the snout pick up tiny electrical charges given off by all living animals. Thus, the shark can "home in" on prey that might be otherwise hidden.

Finally, the great white shark has a good sense of smell. The nostrils are located at the tip of the snout, just above the mouth. About seventy percent of a shark's brain is used to figure out what its nostrils are smelling. The smallest bit of blood in the water can draw a crowd of great whites.

A streamlined body

The best engineers couldn't improve on the great white shark's body. It's as streamlined as a torpedo, and glides through the water with fluid grace. The tail fin, shaped like a new moon, drives the huge body. The shark's "backbone" extends into the tail, giving the tail great strength. As a result, the great white is one of the fastest fish in the sea.

Sharks have large pectoral fins.

The great white has several other fins to keep the huge body in balance. The most important are the pectoral and dorsal fins.

The pectoral fins stick out on each side of the shark, similar to the wings of an airplane. By changing the angle of these fins, the shark can roll to the side or move up and down.

Two dorsal fins appear on the shark's back. These fins keep the fish steady in the water. The larger dorsal fin looks like a triangle. Many people expect to see this fin cutting the water when the shark is attacking. That doesn't always happen! A great white shark can attack from almost any position.

Even on the inside, the great white is well designed. It makes up for not having a swim bladder by having a very large liver. In a two thousand pound (900 kg) shark, this soft organ can weigh up to five hundred pounds (226 kg). Filled with light oil, the liver helps keep the shark from sinking. The oil also provides energy when the shark cannot find food.

A fish that never sleeps

Great white sharks never stop moving. Only forward motion keeps water moving across their gills. If they do stop, their gills can't get oxygen from the water. As a result, great whites don't sleep like other animals do. They just slow down. This fact also explains why no great whites are living in captivity. If one is captured, it stops swimming and sinks to the bottom of its tank. Within a day or so, it dies. No one is sure why great whites "give up" when captured.

Marine biologists remind us that this behavior isn't a problem in the ocean. Indeed, they believe that the great white shark is the perfect predator.

CHAPTER TWO:

The great white shark is at home in all of the world's oceans. With water covering over seventy percent of the earth's surface, these hungry predators turn up almost everywhere.

No one knows how many great white sharks are alive today. Marine biologists, who study them, believe that they aren't very common. One count showed that of every four thousand sharks killed in Florida waters, only one was a great white. Some experts, in fact, believe that too many great whites are being killed. They say that this fearful predator may be an endangered species.

No one knows how many great whites are prowling the oceans of the world.

A varied habitat

Sharks, like all fish and reptiles, are cold-blooded. A cold-blooded animal cannot control its body temperature. Most sharks, as well as most other fish, lose body heat through their gills. The great white shark and a few other members of its family, however, have developed a better system. As their hearts pump, their bloodstream picks up and holds heat given off by their muscles. Thus, great whites can stay active in the cold, deep water. One great white, for example, was hooked and caught at a depth of four thousand feet (1,220 m). Oceans are very cold at that depth. Even so, great whites seem to prefer shallower seas closer to the equator. Most sightings of these sharks are made in warm waters. However, they are found in both cold and warm oceans.

Most great whites prefer warm, shallow seas.

Off North America's Atlantic coast, the great white shark has been seen from Newfoundland to the Gulf of Mexico. In the Pacific, great whites have been spotted from Alaska south to Mexico. The waters off South Africa and Australia are also popular with great whites.

With no fixed habitat, great whites can move around a lot. The sharks swim closer to shore in summer, and move further out during the winter. And they travel great distances. In order to study the great white's movements, scientists have put tags on them. This is a dangerous task for both the scientists and the shark. Great whites put up such a fight when they're caught that a tagged shark often dies soon afterward. If it survives the struggle, the shark leaves the area in a hurry. Swimming at ten miles per hour (16 kph), a great white can travel over a thousand miles (1,600 km) in five days! One great white, tagged off Great Britain, turned up near Canada a year later. A second shark, tagged at the same time, was later found in South American waters.

A hungry hunter

When a great white shark moves in, it takes over the territory. If there are divers in the area, they will see the same shark day after day. The great white allows smaller sharks to share the area only if they do not compete for food. Smaller sharks must catch fish while the great white isn't looking. They also dart in to eat the leftovers from the great white's meals. Great white sharks enforce their "rules" by attacking other sharks. The resulting battles often leave both sharks deeply scarred.

Some marine biologists believe that great white sharks are always hungry. No fish or ocean mammal, large or small, is safe from attack. For the most part, however, sharks prey on weak, old, and sick fish. Like vultures, they also clean up the sea's dead and dying animals. A great white that follows a school of tuna doesn't attack the younger, stronger fish. But if a slower, weaker fish drops behind, the great white flashes in to make a kill.

Almost anything that comes along will serve as food for the great white shark. Their powerful stomach acids digest bones and shells, as well as meat. They eat dead fish, poisonous fish, sea turtles, and large clams. A fully-grown great white can even swallow a one-hundred-pound (45 kg) sea turtle! Nothing seems to give sharks a stomachache.

One old myth says that sharks eat their own weight in fish every day. The great white, however, eats only about fifteen percent of its body weight each week. For a typical great white, that's about five hundred pounds (225 kg) of food per week. Older sharks eat less than young ones. For all their hungry ways, great white sharks sometimes pass by

This great white came out of the water to get a chunk of meat put out by scientists.

an easy meal. No one knows for sure why they ignore one fish — or skin diver — but strike at the next.

The great white shark hunts wherever it finds food. Great whites dive down to snap up bottom swimmers, such as rockfish, stingrays, and octopus. They also take fish that swim near the surface, such as mackerel and tuna. In between, they're just as likely to make a meal of other sharks. One fifteen-foot (4.6 m) great white was found with two six-foot (1.8 m) brown sharks in its stomach.

Are humans ever safe?

Most people, however, don't worry about sharks eating other sharks. They worry about sharks eating

Great whites might attack anything that looks like food.

people. Are those worries based on fact or myth? The answer is somewhere in between. Great white sharks do have a bloody record. In 1916, for example, one great white killed four people off the coast of New Jersey. In one case, the shark swam up a creek to kill its victim. Great whites will attack almost anything. One angry shark even took a bite out of a fishing boat.

Each year seems to turn up a new story. In 1964, a man lost a leg to a great white shark off Australia. Four years later, he went swimming and was attacked again. This time, a shark bit off his wooden leg! In 1976, a diver off the California coast lost both legs to a great white. His life was saved when the shark spit him out. Lifeguards guessed that the shark didn't like the rubbery taste of his wet suit.

Thus, the "Jaws" stories are based on fact. Even so, great white sharks don't seem to go out of their way to attack people. Marine biologists remind us that we're the ones who are invading the shark's habitat. They believe that attacks on humans happen mostly by accident. For example, experts think that great whites attack surfboards because they look like floating sea lions when seen from below. A surfer that paddles to pick up speed looks even more like a swimming sea lion to a hungry great white.

A biologist studies a great white from the safety of a steel cage.

Marine biologists can tell you a lot about the life cycle of most sharks. When it comes to the great white shark, however, they're much less certain. No one has ever seen a great white shark give birth, for example. Great whites die when captured, and watching them in their natural habitat is a risky business. Much of what is known about the great white, therefore, is based on bits of information collected over many years. As far as the experts can tell, great white sharks follow a life cycle that is similar to that of other large sharks.

Let's follow a great white as it begins life in the ocean depths near Florida.

Biologists still have much to learn about the great white.

Born to kill

The female great white swam slowly, sharp teeth showing in her wide mouth. Fourteen feet (4.3 m) long and weighing more than a ton, she was a scary sight. Inside that huge body, she carried a litter of pups (young sharks) ready to be born. The large, active pups had grown in eggsacs. The female had mated with a male great white months earlier.

One male pup was larger than the others. Still unborn, it already felt hungry. Blindly, it took a bite out of a nearby pup. Then it ate its smaller "brother." A few days later, the litter was born. Each pup was about four feet (1.2 m) long and weighed over thirty pounds (13.6 kg).

The pups swam away as soon as they were born. That was their only choice. The female might have eaten them if they came too close to her hungry mouth. The large male pup was driven by instincts passed on by its ancestors. Its brain responded to messages from its keen senses. Within the first hour, it caught and ate an injured stingray.

The large pup soon found a territory of its own. Day by day, it hunted and ate well. Once a female from the same litter tried to enter the territory. The male pup quickly drove her away. Great whites never hunt or travel together. If one became hungry, it would attack the other.

Marine biologists can only guess how long the

great white pups will live. Some experts think that a great white may live thirty years or more. If a great white is captured, its teeth don't tell anything. Young or old, shark teeth look much alike. Marine biologists can use the scales of some bony fish to tell the fish's age. But the sharp denticles on the shark's skin don't give any clues at all.

The feeding frenzy

The young great white male was growing fast. It picked up its first scars later that year. A fishing boat dumped a load of dead, chopped up fish into the water. Sharks of all kinds from miles around soon gathered at the feeding spot. The blood in the water, plus their own numbers, drove them into a feeding frenzy. The young great white drove into the pack, snapping at everything within reach. Other sharks bit back, ripping its tough skin. All control gone, the sharks slashed at everything within reach.

The most terrible feeding frenzies happen when injured people fall into the water after a shipwreck. Drawn by the scent of blood, many sharks soon gather at the spot. As the feeding frenzy grows, more and more sharks arrive. The wildly biting sharks often rip their helpless victims to shreds.

Sharks are drawn by the scent of blood.

A loner with few enemies

The change of the seasons sent the great white shark closer to shore. Larger and stronger, it was no longer a pup. It seemed to like the warm offshore water during the summer months. The other great whites in the litter had gone their own ways. Some set off on migrations to the waters off Europe and South America. Each preferred to live away from others of its own kind.

The great white wasn't completely alone. Two kinds of smaller fish kept it company. A swarm of pilot fish lived off bits of fish left behind when the shark fed. The pilot fish were allowed to swim almost into the shark's mouth. The shark never ate any of them. Perhaps great whites don't like the taste of these small fish. The second "free-loaders" were six remora. These two-foot (61 cm) long fish were fastened to the shark by suction discs on their heads. Like the pilot fish, the remora fed on scraps from the shark's food.

The great white male reached full size in its sixth year. Aside from people, parasites, and other sharks, no other sea creature would attack it. When it was still small, however, the young great white had a narrow escape. A fifteen-foot (4.6 m) swordfish

Two types of fish keep the great white shark company: the pilot (left) and the remora.

speared it with its "sword." The sharp point drew blood, but the shark twisted free and escaped. On another day, porpoises saved a sailor whose boat sank in the great white's territory. The sailor's splashing drew the shark's attention. However, several porpoises drove the shark away. Instead of biting, they butted the shark with their hard snouts.

The other great white pups were not so lucky. One eight-foot (2.4 m) female was swallowed by a sperm whale. Another was grabbed by a giant squid. A third pup was eaten by a thirty-foot (9 m) crocodile along the coast of South America. The crocodile swallowed the shark in one gulp.

Mating completes the life cycle

When the great white shark was fully grown, it was ready to mate. The male found a female swimming near the Florida Keys. As in most species of shark, she was larger than he was. The mating game was a violent one. The male circled the female, biting hard at her back and sides. When they were ready to mate, they swam side-by-side. Male sharks have an organ near their tails called a clasper. The clasper entered the female's body to leave sperm to fertilize her eggs. When the mating was finished, the female swam away. The male never saw the pups that were born many months later.

The male great white lived only a few more weeks. Off the Bahamas one day, it struck at a shiny fish that caught its attention. As it bit down, a sharp hook caught in the upper part of its mouth. Up on the surface, the crew of a fishing boat got ready to pull in their catch. The sea's greatest predator had met its match.

The male great white is usually smaller than the female.

CHAPTER FOUR:

People who like to eat fish often say that they would never eat shark. The thought of eating a predator that feeds on people makes these folks feel a little sick.

However, many people have eaten shark without knowing it. Seafood stores have been known to sell shark steaks under names like "red snapper." Shark flesh is firm and tasty, like that of a swordfish. Fish-catching people in many parts of the world learned that fact centuries ago.

A treasure chest in the past

Some Pacific island natives thought that sharks were gods. Their priests sometimes threw people to the hungry "gods" to keep them happy. More often, the natives hunted the great white and other sharks. They caught the dangerous fish with their spears, hooks, and boiled melons!

The "melon trick" was a clever one. The people cooked the melons for hours, until the inner juices were boiling. Then they threw the hot melons, covered with bits of fish, into the sea. When the sharks swallowed the melons, the melons burst and the hot juices and steam killed them. Filled with gases, the bodies floated to the surface. Then the natives could easily collect them.

Almost every part of the great white shark and its many cousins was good for something. Pacific islanders ate the flesh and used the oil from the liver. They also lined the edges of their wooden clubs with the sharp teeth. Kings and priests wore the teeth of the great white as a symbol of power. Even shark skin was useful — once the denticles were scraped off. Experts say that leather made from shark skin is much stronger than cowhide.

Fishing for the great white today

Today most of the people who catch great white sharks do so for sport. Anglers (people who fish for sport) like to go after the biggest game they can find — and the great white shark is big! No license is needed, since sharks aren't protected by any laws. The anglers can't go out to sea in a rowboat, however. They must hire a fishing boat and its crew.

They need the crew to run the boat and to help bring their catch on board.

The anglers drop their heavy fishing lines in an area where great whites are known to feed. They bait the hooks with large pieces of fish. The bait leaves the smell of blood in the water. If any great whites are in the area, they will come to check out the scent. The sharks don't always take the bait. They may prefer to feed on whole fish, or perhaps they're warned by the sight of the fishing line.

A great white strikes a bait!

If a great white shark does strike the bait, it usually runs away from the boat at high speed. The line zips out from the reel so fast it must be cooled with water. Some crews tie an oil drum to the line to act as a float. Pulling the drum through the water helps tire the shark.

The great white often runs with the bait for a hundred yards (91 m) before swallowing it. Then the shark makes a second run, fighting the pull of the line and the float. The battle may last for hours. The angler and the boat crew work together to keep the line tight without snapping it. At the same time, they try not to let the shark rest. That's harder to do than it sounds. After hours of fighting a great white, the angler's arms feel as though they're ready to break.

Time of greatest danger

Finally, the tired angler pulls the equally tired shark next to the boat. The crew members stand ready with a hooked spear called a gaff. They shove the gaff into the shark's back near the head. Great whites aren't used to being attacked, so the gaff leaves them stunned. That gives the crew time to tie a second line around the shark's tail.

The time of greatest danger is when the crew start to pull the great white out of the water. A shark

Bringing the shark into the boat is very dangerous!

Great whites are lifted into the boat by the tail.

doesn't give up easily. The huge fish whips its body from side to side, trying to break the rope. One blow from the tail can knock someone out. At the same time, the shark is snapping at everything in sight.

Slowly, the crew members lift the great white onto the deck of the boat. One sailor has the job of killing the shark by hitting it on its head with a club. Even so, the crew still treat "Jaws" with great respect. If someone reaches in to take out the hook too soon, the mouth may snap shut. The razor-sharp teeth could easily take off an arm. Everyone who handles the rough-skinned body also wears heavy gloves.

A market for great whites

Fish experts say the flesh of the great white tastes better than that of other sharks. The Japanese, for example, grind it up and make it into fish cakes. In addition, people make leather from the skin and use the liver for its oil. Known as squalene, the oil is used for treating burns. It's also used to make lipstick! Some scientists have studied squalene as a possible cure for cancer and other diseases. Some cancer victims treated with squalene have improved, but no one knows if the shark oil really cured them.

Tourists, on the other hand, like to buy the teeth. A set of jaws from a great white sells for around a thousand dollars (U.S.). The teeth are also made into necklaces and bracelets.

Marine biologists watch this and worry that too many great whites are being caught. They'd rather study these giant predators than harm them. After all, they say, there are many more sharks killed by people than people killed by sharks.

CHAPTER FIVE:

Some people believe that humans will someday live in undersea cities. If that's true, tomorrow's people will have the great white shark as a neighbor.

Little by little, marine biologists are finding ways to study and control the great white. Only when we know much more about our new neighbor can we safely move in next door.

Life in a shark cage

The only way to study the great white shark is to join it under water. Marine biologists know better than to dive too closely to the great whites, however. They go down in cages made from steel bars and wire mesh. The cages are big enough to hold one or two divers and hang by cables from a boat above. When a cage is used to study smaller sharks, the bars are made from hollow aluminum tubes. But the great white is another matter. For these giants, the divers are behind heavy steel bars.

Great white sharks don't seem to notice the steel bars. The sharks often swim straight at the cage, mouths wide open. A shark hitting the cage at thirty miles an hour (48 kph) sends it swinging wildly. The great whites sometimes bite at the bars, trying to get at the people inside. The bars usually bend from the force of the attack. At times, those sharp teeth are only inches away from the diver's face!

Studying the great white

Marine biologists have done many tests from the safety of the cages. In one test, they released small amounts of blood into the water to test the shark's sense of smell. The great whites easily zeroed in on one part blood to ten million parts water! The divers also watched from their cages as sharks gathered to rip apart a dead sperm whale that the biologists had found. They were able to safely film the feeding frenzy that followed. They saw how the great whites and other frenzied sharks bit and tore at each other, as well as the whale.

Some beautiful action pictures have been made of great whites from the shark cages. The divers use waterproof cameras and lights. The lights must be very bright, and the film must be very sensitive to catch the great whites in their dim, deep water habitat. The lights frighten some fish, but not the great white shark. The best motion picture on the great white ever made, *Blue Water, White Death* was filmed in this way.

Protection from shark attack

Shark cages are good for studying sharks up close. But what about swimmers, divers, and the victims of shipwrecks? We can't put a shark cage around everyone who goes into the ocean.

Pacific island natives used to put smelly oils into the water in hopes that sharks would stay away. They also tried making clicking noises to scare the sharks. Later, divers released curtains of air bubbles to scare off the predators. A few people even claim that a shark will back off if you punch it in the nose!

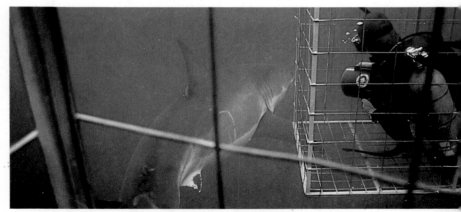

Biologists are protected by using a steel cage.

In any case, these tactics only work with smaller sharks.

Scientists have long looked for a chemical shark repellent to keep sharks away. Like the island natives, they believe that great whites and other sharks dislike certain smells. As a starting point, the scientists knew that sharks would not feed on the rotten flesh of a dead shark. They learned that the flesh contains acetic acid. They tried adding different chemicals to the acetic acid. None of the mixes kept sharks away. Finally, a colored dye was added and "Shark Chaser" was born.

The dye in Shark Chaser caused most sharks to stay away, at least for awhile. Sailors and air crews carried the repellent with them during World War II. If their ship or plane went down at sea, they were often able to protect themselves. The flyers also carried a "Shark Screen." This is a large plastic bag which is held up by three air-filled rings. Once inside the bag, the swimmer cannot be seen or smelled by nearby sharks. The brightly-colored rings also made it easier for a rescue plane to spot the downed flyer.

Scientists now know that it was only the dye in Shark Chaser that stopped shark attacks, because the sharks couldn't see their victims. Recently, however, scientists have found some chemicals that seem to repel sharks. But, if you ever see a shark while you're swimming, you probably won't have any shark repellent with you. What should you do?

Experts say, "Stay Calm." Too much splashing may attract the shark. Swim slowly back to shore.

In South Africa and Australia, nets have been set up to keep sharks away from the beaches. Sharks that try to swim through the nets catch their gills in the mesh. Trapped in the net, the sharks die. Shark attacks near Sydney, Australia dropped to zero after the nets were put up. The nets are costly to put up and repair, but they do save lives.

Should we kill the killer?

When people and wildlife mix, nothing is ever simple. Conservationists worry about the effect of the beach protection nets on other sea life. In Queensland, Australia, more than twenty thousand sharks died in the nets in just sixteen years. But the nets also killed harmless dugongs, porpoises, and sea turtles. Conservationists also point out that only a few of the sharks were dangerous to people. Most of the sharks were types that do not attack people.

Should the great white shark be protected? Marine biologists like to remind us that the great white shark is part of the balance of nature. And almost anyone can admire the beauty and grace of these deadly killers. Most surfers and swimmers, however, find that beauty hard to see. Few of them are likely to set up a Great White Shark Society to protect this shark.

Hopefully, someone will figure out a way for people and sharks to exist together. But until better ways of protecting people are found, we would be better off if we just learned to stay away from nature's largest underwater predator whenever possible.

Hopefully, a way will soon be found to protect people from great whites.

INDEX/GLOSSARY:

PLANKTON 10 — *Tiny plants and animals that live in lakes and oceans.*

PREDATOR 8, 10, 16, 17, 32, 33, 39, 42, 44 — *An animal that lives by preying on other animals.*

PREY 5, 13, 14, 20 — *Animals that are usually eaten by larger animals.*

PRIMITIVE 8 — *Animals and plants that have not changed through the years.*

PUP 9, 27, 29, 31, 32 — *A newly born great white shark.*

SENSORY PORES 14 — *Small openings in a shark's snout that help detect its prey.*

SHARK CAGE 40, 41, 42 — *A box made of steel bars and wire mesh which protects divers who are studying the great white shark.*

SHARK REPELLENT 43 — *Any chemical that keeps sharks away from people in the water.*

SNOUT 14, 31 — *The part of an animal's head that sticks out in front and contains the nose.*

SPERM 32 — *The fluid which the male releases inside the female to fertilize her eggs.*

SQUALENE 39 — *The oil made from the large liver of a shark.*

SWIM BLADDER 9 — *The organ in a fish which helps it float, even when it's not swimming.*

WILDLIFE
HABITS & HABITAT

READ AND ENJOY THE SERIES:

If you would like to know more about all kinds of wildlife, you should take a look at the other books in this series.

You'll find books on bald eagles and other birds. Books on alligators and other reptiles. There are books about deer and other big-game animals. And there are books about sharks and other creatures that live in the ocean.

In all of the books you will learn that life in the wild is not easy. But you will also learn what people can do to help wildlife survive. So read on!